[The] Swede

By Christer Amnéus
Illustrations by Bo Zaunders

[The] Swede

Not too little and not too much
The Very Unofficial guide to the Swedes
From A – Z and beyond

Christer Amnéus

NORDSTJERNAN
Förlag, New York

Nordstjernan Förlag, New York 2020
800.827.9333

[The] Swede
Copyright © Christer Amnéus and Nordstjernan, 2020
Cover photo: iStockphoto
Cover design: Nadia Marks Wojcik
Illustrations: Bo Zaunders
ISBN: 978-0-9968460-8-0
First U.S. Edition, January 2020
Printed in the USA

Culture, ethnic background, geography and history may divide, but languages unite.

The British Council estimates that English is spoken at a useful level by approximately 1.75 billion people, in other words by a quarter of the world's population (The Guardian, UK) That is why this book is written in English and not in Swedish, the language of about 10 million individuals, including the author.

We all live in an ever-changing world. This means that by the time you read this book, facts and information may be totally out of date. Still, the essence remains.

Nordstjernan Förlag
Book Services
PO Box 1710
New Canaan CT 06840
www.nordstjernan.com

Hej!

The above is quite possibly the most commonly used word in Sweden. You say "Hej" (pronounced hey) when you meet someone. That goes for everybody, including His Majesty the King and any politician, tycoon or celebrity.

Swedes are very informal and would never say "God dag" or anything like that. Of course "God morgon" or "God kväll/God afton" (good evening) are accepted, but can easily be avoided. They may be used on television or by the staff of a restaurant.

Among young people "Tjenare" is a colloquial way of putting it, even "Tjabba". But refrain from using them. You are not 15 anymore or am I wrong? Also, remember "god" means "good". "Gud" means "God". With these words it is time to say a little about what to expect from the pages you are about to encounter.

This book ...

... was written with the intent of introducing Sweden and the Swedes to English-speaking people. I also wanted to keep the level of English fairly simple so it would be accessible to non-native English speakers. Originally the idea was spawned by the questions from all the interesting guests I have had the pleasure of getting to know. The time I have spent in Britain or the USA has made me reflect upon my native country. This has given me a chance to embark on a ship of observation.

Naturally with my prejudices, preconceived ideas, personal experiences, friends and other Swedes, as seen on TV, portrayed in books and listened to on the bus, I have come to the conclusions on which this book is based. Of course other Swedes may totally disagree with my opinions.

We also included a section in the back from Nordstjernan — an addendum where we list the 100 most influential Swedes of the second millennium. With a population until a few years ago of less than ten million, Sweden has had a remarkable influence on the rest of the world. Without getting into why or how we wanted you to have our biased view of who.

My aim has been to keep it at a personal and informal level. The reader can go through it at random, starting in the middle going backward or forward. Since the order is alphabetical it will be like doing something spontaneously. Housewives, Hugging, Humor, and Husesyn (House inspection) will appear in that order, if you can call that order. The book can be read in your home country before leaving or before not going at all. You can keep it in a pocket or in your smart phone and read bits and pieces on sightseeing boats, in museum queues or in hotel rooms.

This is a light-hearted book, with the occasional tinge of seriousness, and has absolutely no pretensions. All I want to give you is my picture of this diversified country that I love so much.

Good luck!
And most of all, Välkommen till Sverige!

Christer Amnéus

About the author

The writer of this book has in his selfish way reserved the paragraphs in this book to dispose as he wishes. He takes almost full responsibility for the information in this book. The intent has been to entertain and inform in a less serious way. Do not judge the poor soul too hard, if facts have changed since the book's birth or if texts have faults, due to lack of intelligence or knowledge. And, mind you, the writer is a Swedish citizen, who has never lived in an English-speaking country, only visited some of them. So pardon the language in its sometime Swenglish shape.

Christer Amnéus used to teach English and German at an upper secondary school (students aged 16–19). He has published numerous books for educational use throughout his more than 40 years in the classroom. Added to that, also some 40 manuscripts for the Swedish Educational Radio.

Another important part of his career has been scripts for cabarets, a number of acts for entertainment use and lyrics for light pop music.

Table of Contents

ABBA	23
Absolut	23
Accents and dialects	23
Addressing people	24
Advent	25
Allemansrätten	25
Allotment System, the	27
Allsång på Skansen	27
Allt för Sverige	28
Allvar och melankoli (Seriousness and Melancholy)	29
Alvar (the landform)	30
Anglo-Saxon phenomena	31
Animal life	31
Art	32
Arv (inheritance)	33
Aquavit	33
Bag-in-box	33
Bail (Borgen)	34
Bananas	34
Banks and post offices	34
Bathrooms	35
Beauty	36
Beggars	36
Bergman, Ingemar	37
Bergvärme (Thermal heating)	37
Berries and mushrooms	37
Birds	38
Blekinge	39
Blonds	39
Boasting	39
Bohuslän	40

Table of Contents

Boring Swedes	40
Boys and girls	41
Breakfast	42
Breastfeeding	42
Business meetings	42
Candy	43
Cars (Automobiles)	43
Cashless Sweden	44
Celebrities	44
Cell phones	45
Cemeteries	46
Children	46
Children's names	47
Christmas	48
Climate	49
Coffee	49
Conservatories (Sunrooms)	50
Costumes	50
Crayfish parties	50
Dagens (lunch)	52
Dagny	52
Dalarna	52
Dalsland	53
Deadlines	54
Decisions	54
Delaware	54
Did you know this about Sweden?	54
Dial-a-Swede	55
Disabled, the	56
Discussions	56
DNA	57

Table of Contents

Doors	57
Drink and drive	58
Drugstores	58
Easter	58
Eating	59
Economy	59
Edible Country	60
Electricity	60
Electronics	60
Emigration	62
Equality	62
EU	64
Eurovision Song Contest	64
Exchange students	64
Expressions	65
Facts and figures	66
Fake news	67
Family names	68
Faucets (Taps)	69
Feminism	69
Ferries	69
Fiftieth birthday	69
Fika	71
First lesson of Swedish Grammar	71
Fishballs (Fiskbullar)	72
Flags	74
Flogsta scream, the	74
Flygskam (Flight-shaming)	74
Folk music	76
Folk parks	76
Food	76

Table of Contents

Fredagsmys (Cosy Friday)	78
Genealogy	78
Generalizations	79
Gingerbread house	79
God	79
Gothenburg (Göteborg)	80
Gotland	81
Greta	82
Gästrikland	83
Halland	83
HBTQ	84
H&M	84
Hej	85
Hej då	201
Hen	85
Hollywood stars (Swedish)	85
Homes	86
Houses	88
Housewives	88
Hugging	89
Humor	89
Husesyn (House inspection)	90
Hälsingland	90
Härjedalen	91
Ice-cream	91
Ikea	91
Immigration	92
Internet	93
Inventions and discoveries	93
iPads (and other electronic devices) at school	95
Jordgubbar (Strawberries)	95

Table of Contents

Jämtland	95
Kalles kaviar	96
Kilometers and miles	97
Kilos and pounds	98
Kings and Queens	98
Knäckebröd	101
Korvkiosk	101
Lagom	102
Language, the Swedish	102
Lappland (Lapland)	103
Letters to the editor	103
Lindgren, Astrid	104
Lingonberries	104
Liquorice, salty	104
Literature	105
Liters	105
Lobster premiere	106
Loppis (Flea market)	106
Lucia	106
Läxrut	108
Lördagsgodis (Saturday candy)	108
Making fun	109
Map	197, 199
Medelpad	109
Mentality	110
#MeToo	111
Midnight sun	111
Midsummer	111
Migration 2015	112
Military defense	113
Milk	113

Table of Contents

Moberg, Vilhelm	114
Mobile preschools	114
Modern Myths	115
Moose	116
Music	117
Muslims	117
Myself	118
Narcotics	119
National Day	120
Nationalism	120
Nature	122
Neutrality	122
News and weather on TV	122
Newspapers	123
No	123
Nobel Prize, the	123
Nordic companies	124
Norrbotten	125
Närke	125
Old towns	126
Order	126
Osvensk (un-Swedish)	126
Page Three	127
Palme, Olof	127
Parental leave	128
Parties	128
Permissiveness	130
Personnummer	131
Pets	131
PISA results	132
Pitch-accent language	132

Table of Contents

Polar bears	133
Polar Music Prize, the	133
Police	133
Politeness	134
Politics	136
Poor country	136
Prehistoric Sweden and onwards	137
Prices	137
P-skiva	138
Q-numbers (Queuing)	138
Raggare	139
Rea	139
Realtors	139
Recycling	140
Religion	142
Royal family	143
Sami people	144
Saturday night	144
School	144
Security freaks	146
Sharing bedrooms	146
Showers	147
Similar words with different meanings 111	147
Skåne	148
Slums	150
Small talk	150
Smoking	151
Småland	151
Smörgås	152
Smörgåsbord	152
Smörgåstårta	153

Table of Contents

Snus	154
Sommarstuga	154
Songwriters	155
Spanking	156
Speaking English	156
Sport	156
Spotify	157
State, the welfare	157
Stavgång	158
Staying in someone's home	158
Stockholm	159
Stockholm, I m from ...	160
Stores	161
Strindberg, August	162
Studenten	162
Stuga	163
Suck it, baby	164
Surströmming	164
Svensktoppen	165
Svensson	165
SWEA	166
Swearwords	166
Sweden best country in the world	166
Swedes pronouncing ...	168
Swedish Sin	168
Swimming	169
Systembolaget	170
Södermanland	170
Taciturn Northerners	171
Tack	171
Tattoos	172

Table of Contents

Taube, Evert	172
Telephoning	172
Television	173
Thermometer scales	173
Threats to society	173
Time	174
Tipping	174
Titles	175
Tourism in Sweden	175
Towns	175
Trade unions	176
Traffic	176
Treriksröset	177
Tricky Swedish words	178
Tubes	179
TV	180
Uppland	182
Vabba	183
Vacation	183
Vasa, Gustav	184
Ven and Visingsö	184
Vikings	185
Visitors	185
Vägtull (Toll roads)	186
Värmland	186
Västerbotten	186
Västergötland	188
Västmanland	189
Walks	189
Wall-to-wall carpets	190
Walpurgis Night	190

West Coast, the	190
Windows	191
Young in Sweden	192
Ångermanland	192
Öland	193
Öresundsbron	193
Östergötland	194
Översättning (Translation)	195
Map of Sweden, including "Landskap"	197
Official map of Sweden, with "Län"	199
That's it …	201

Addendum

The 100 Most Influential Swedes	205
The hall of twenty	208
Historical heavyweights	211
The literati	213
Stage and screen	215
The musicians	216
The artists	217
The wide world of sports	218
The politicians	219
The world of business	220
Also considered	221

ABBA

Nearly 400 million records have been sold by this Swedish popular music phenomenon. Other surveys claim only half that number. This tendency to have that large gap in numbers goes for most other artists.

ABBA's long history in music as a group covers 47 years (1972-2019) so far, and their chart successes still continue. They have had 10 singles in the Billboard Top 20 in USA, 20 altogether in the Hot 100, four albums in the Top 20, all in all 13 on the Billboard Top 200, not including the number one album Mamma Mia, and Mamma Mia! Here We Go Again reaching number three.

In the UK their success is even greater. Nine singles and nine albums in the number one spot demonstrate this. Added to that, Mamma Mia! Here We Go Again also got to number one and Mamma Mia reached number five. As of mid 2019 the album ABBA Gold had stayed 900 weeks in the UK Top 100, the second largest seller after Queen. The group disbanded in 1982, long after the two married couples had broken up, but their music can be heard all over today. Thank you for the music, ABBA.

Absolut

The Swedish trademark Absolut Vodka has spread worldwide. This strong alcohol in its icy bottle is sold in dozens of countries and is probably one of the biggest successes ever of a single Swedish product. Visiting Americans have been amazed that such a large brand name comes from such a small distillery in Sweden (now owned by Pernod Ricard).

Accents and dialects

The various parts of the country have their own way of pronouncing words and their local vocabularies. Normally local Swedes understand each other quite well, be it a Northerner making conversation with a Southerner or an Easterner with a Westerner, not without exceptions, though.

Stockholm has got what many native Swedes would describe as correct Swedish. It is in fact a mixture of accents, influenced by various parts of the country that have affected and shaped it in this melting pot. Others would argue that people in Södermanland (especially the town of Nyköping) or possibly Uppland speak "correct" Swedish.

The Gothenburg (Göteborg) accent and melody differ greatly from the Stockholm accent – and others from central- and east Sweden.

The southern provinces (Halland, Skåne, Blekinge and Småland) have their own provincial stamps on pronunciation. They do not sound at all alike, although a certain common feature exists.

The northern parts of the country contain many accents, which have a certain singing quality to them. The Stockholm lingo has been influenced by them through the great migration to the capital.

Dalarna, Värmland, Gotland and Tornedalen are other examples of provinces (counties) with distinct accents. Finnish and/or Meänkieli (Tornefinska, Torne Valley Finnish) are languages along the Torne River spoken in many homes.

Addressing people

The Swedes are very proud of their habit of calling everyone – and that means everyone in the country – by their first names. It all started in the late 1960s when a high official put a sign on his office door saying "Säg gärna du" ("Call me by my first name if you please"). All of a sudden you would address Olof Palme with "Hej Olof!" instead of "Good morning, Mr. Palme/Prime Minister!" The idea caught on rapidly and became a natural part of everyday life.

There is one exception, though. When addressing the King and the Queen directly you would say, "Will the King agree to this" or "Has the Queen anything to add?" His or Her Highness would not be used. As for princesses and princes, reporters tend to forget who they are and simply say "du."

A tendency to go back to the old system (saying "ni" and not "du") exists in posh Stockholm shops and possibly in banks or similar institutions in the country. Especially young people seem to favor this way of distinguishing between friends and family and others. As a tourist you should choose the "du" form.

Advent

In the rectangular Advent candleholder you have four candles, moss and small decorations like artificial lingonberries. On the First of Advent the first candle is lit and then another one each consecutive Sunday. By the time Christmas is knocking on the door, the fourth and last candle will be burning along with the other three.

Most windows in homes will have differently shaped electrical Advent candles, preferably with seven lights. Over the years, the number of these decorations can be said to have increased incredibly and have even spread across the North Sea and started selling in the UK. In offices and public buildings electrical Advent candles come in numerous shapes and huge numbers.

They light up the December darkness and make life tolerable. No saving of electricity here. The Advent star shines in most homes as well. It may come in wood, metal or any other material and hangs from the ceiling or in windows as a reminder of Christmas and the birth of Christ.

Allemansrätten (Right of Public Access)

"That is communism. I'd shoot every one trespassing on my land," a Swedish-American cousin exclaimed in reference to the idea of the right to roam.

The right of access to rivers, forests, meadows and mountains has its origin in previous centuries. You are allowed to pick berries or mushrooms on the owner's land and you may even pitch a tent for one night (not near a house or in someone's garden of course).

This right has deep roots and is seldom violated by native Swedes. The burning of fires or leaving rubbish will not be tolerated. To respect and treasure nature is so obvious to the inhabitants.

Unfortunately there are a few continental cousins, who are known for their ability to abuse the Right of Public Access. Farmers have woken up to find a caravan or mobile home next to their barn, or tents in the front garden, even tourists picking lettuce or carrots. Native residents complain in the local papers about foreign tourists sealing off part of the beach for their own purposes. Canoe safaris have also destroyed valuable riverbanks.

Allemansrätten. NOT about guardening your own property, more or less the opposite. As long as it's not part of someone's back yard, in Sweden you have the freedom to roam even on other people's land.

Allotment system, the

This was a system used in Sweden in order to keep a trained army at all times. It came into use in the last part of the European Thirty Years' War (in the 1640s), and was not replaced until 1901 when the Swedish Armed Forces Conscription System was introduced. Two different allotment systems, the old and the new, were in use in Sweden. The soldiers in the new allotment were known as "croft soldiers" (indelta soldater), due to the small crofts allotted to them. These cottages often housed large families and sometimes even cattle.

Contracts forcing counties and provinces to raise and supply a regiment of 1,000 or 1,200 men in both wartime and peacetime were written. Usually, four farms formed a unit, given the task of equipping one soldier. Those farms, known as the rote, also provided a croft (soldattorp), farmland, supplies and equipment for the soldier. He could make a military career, provided he survived the hardship of war. The rest of the men could continue being farmers and crofters. The soldier's duty was to attend military drills, and in time of war join the army, where soldiers died in large numbers of disease and sometimes by bullets.

Allsång på Skansen

The art of the sing-along has a strong following in Sweden, regardless of generations. In the summer a weekly televised show, Allsång på Skansen, takes place at Skansen (the centrally located Stockholm park has an outdoor museum and a zoo) and comprises all kinds of music, from traditional songs to rock, pop, rap and house music. Domestic and international stars perform and the crowd of 10,000 or more adults, youngsters and children go crazy in Blowing in the Wind, Let it Be, Waterloo, or whatever the producers decide to include in the show.

Allt för Sverige

In the television show "Allt för Sverige" (also known as The Great Swedish Adventure), 10 Americans of Swedish ancestry are selected to take part in a trip around Sweden which includes a competition in which they are eliminated one by one each week. The show is informative and fun and the Americans are also presented with strange facts (like in this book). Two examples are: Swedes don't talk to their neighbors.They are subject to Murphy's Law. Who would believe this?

Allsång på Skansen. Skansen, the world's oldest open-air museum in Stockholm, founded in 1891, is known for its family friendly zoo and the summers' sing-alongs (not by the inhabitants of the zoo, however)

In one episode the Americans were surprised that people on a street in Älvsbyn, in the far north province of Norrbotten, were not keen to answer their questions. Why? A possible answer: 1) Swedes are not always confident when it comes to speaking English; Remember, English is another language. 2) They thought the attackers were trying to sell mobile phone contracts or something like that.

All in all, this is silly but excellent television. In the last episode of each season (The show started in 2011), the winner gets to meet a great number of his or her Swedish relatives. It is a heartwarming program with tears, laughter, strong feelings and people discovering new sides of their personas. When interviewed, the contestants often express their desire to stay in the land of their ancestors for good, or at least to keep coming back for visits. Despite our differences we are unified in so many aspects of life.

Allvar och melankoli (Seriousness and Melancholy)

August Strindberg, the writer, and Ingmar Bergman, film producer and writer, have produced great art by mixing seriousness and melancholy with darkness. Along with Lars Norén and Karin Boye, the first one playwright among other things and the latter a poet and novelist, their blue feelings have developed into a palette of colors expressing various aspwwects of life. Bergman admitted that some of his films were depressing, although melancholy would no doubt best describe them. What if these big names had been happy all the time? That would not have turned their work into fantastic writing or filmmaking worldwide.

Seriousness could be a mental condition, a streak of melancholy, but also simply a wish to be taken seriously in everyday life. It could also be interpreted differently, like in the two following cases.

There are 27 Swedes called Allvar (seriousness) as their first name.

On top of that we have Allvar, a brand of men´s underwear, where the product is based on fir- and pine tree wood. Can you still take Swedes seriously?

Alvar (Landform)

This is a landform which in fact is a limestone plain with thin soil and sparse grassland vegetation. It can be found in many countries but Sweden holds about 70% of the planet´s area (665 km2 out of 995 km2). Typical of an alvar is the multitude of rare plants and the lack of trees. Three popular alvars exist on the islands of Öland and Gotland and in Västergötland (a western province). In the summer a typical alvar may be as dry as Swedish humor, probably not more.

Allvar och melankoli.

Anglo-Saxon phenomena

The average Swedish resident looks with keen eyes on anything that is Anglo-Saxon. A certain fascination lies behind this interest. To get an opportunity to speak English may be enough to get him or her going, regardless of the visitor's nationality, race or age.

A black American from Harlem, an Indian from Bombay or a sheep farmer from New South Wales will all intrigue any Swede just as long as he speaks some kind of Anglo Saxon lingo or one of its latter day versions.

In today's Sweden, film titles tend not to be translated. That is why Searching, Papillon, Once upon a Time in Hollywood and The Spy Who Dumped Me are called Searching, Papillon, Once upon a Time in Hollywood and The Spy Who Dumped Me in Swedish. Many TV commercials, including those for Hollywood make-up products, use the English language.

Real estate firms may be called Home, pubs The Old Dublin Shamrock, schools The IT College or pop groups First Aid Kit, Icona Pop or Ghost. English is popular and has come to stay. Will it remain important in the European Union after Brexit (and will British students have to learn to speak French and German)?

Animal life

350,000 moose are reduced in number by 100,000 annually in the hunting season in autumn. More than 350 wolves roam around the forests killing animals. They are protected by law but still hated by local sheep farmers and Sami reindeer owners. Approximately 3,000 bears attempt to stay away from mankind in the large forests of Sweden. An estimated 1,000 lynx try to be invisible to the human eye but are said to exist. There are plenty of deer, fowl and smaller life forms in the country. The most feared one is the tick, which causes infections and suffering. It could be described as the most dangerous living creature, ahead of wolves and snakes (vipers and grass snakes). These days families get vaccinated. It takes three shots first, then after three years one and after five years another one. And it goes on like that.

Art

Alexander Roslin, Anders Zorn, Carl Larsson, Bruno Liljefors, Isaac Grünewald, John Bauer, Sigrid Hjertén, Bror Hjort, Peter Dahl and Lars Lerin are Swedish painters. Sculptor Carl Milles and architect Ragnar Östberg (Stockholm Town Hall) have to be included here, too. Their names are all of great influence in Swedish art. But to attempt to deal with art in a publication of this kind is impossible. So why not buy some art books instead?

The bag-in-box (cask wine) has completely changed the habit of wine drinking in Sweden

Arv (inheritance)

"He won't get one single dollar. He's my son, but he has always been the bad apple. I'll leave him no money in my will, but his sister and brother will get a lot." Well, in Sweden that is not possible. Each child of yours must have their share of the will, no matter what. They are entitled to their part of the inheritance. There is no getting away with it. Before you settle down in Sweden as a happy, married parent, be sure to read about this law first.

Aquavit

While wine and craft beer has made serious inroads in Sweden there are still occasions when the bottle of aquavit makes an appearance. Midsummer, crayfish parties and surströmming parties are such occasions. Surströmming, this fermented fish, is so disgusting that we have included a section under Surströmming to warn you. Christmas or a regular smörgåsbord may be accompanied by small schnapps- also called nubbe- shot glasses with Skåne, Herrgårds, Bäsk or any of the provincial specialties. Beware, the drink, which is often downed with a drinking song, is essentially pure but spiced vodka. Avoid making a face in order to show that you are not a newcomer, and also in the hope that it will disappear down your throat as soon as possible.

Bag-in-box

The introduction of the bag-in-box (cask wine) has completely changed the habit of wine drinking in Sweden, and sales are high today. After all, to have a box containing three liters in your kitchen makes it next to impossible to not have at least one glass a day, since it is there anyway. The odd bottle will only last one evening, so what's the point? A bag-in-box is practical, and cheaper. The price is lower, but is the price of your well-being cheap?

Bail (Borgen)

In 2019 an American rap artist, ASAP Rocky, was arrested in Sweden for assault, along with two bodyguards. The American president attempted to interfere, with no success. No wonder, the Swedish civil law system does not accept bail. Everyone, celebrities, criminals, petty thieves, CEOs or refugees are treated fairly, regardless of background. They may have to face one of the three levels that exist, or even all three. 53 district courts (tingsrätter) form the lowest level, then 6 courts of appeals (hovrätter) and finally the Supreme Court of Sweden (Högsta Domstolen) that make out this system. Politicians, from the Prime Minister and down, have no say in these matters. They make laws but do not execute them or interfere. By the way, capital punishment was abolished about 100 years ago. And there is no such thing as life imprisonment in reality. After an appeal it can be lowered to 18 years, which is the maximum sentence in Sweden.

Bananas

Swedes consume more than 35 pounds per person annually. Their closeness to nature may contribute to this taking to bananas. I would not go so far as to say we are a bunch of apes, but man and apes have got more or less the same genes, which might explain some of it. Do not bring a bunch of bananas, however, to the hostess of a party. Flowers will be more appreciated, which is proven by the fact that 150 million tulips are sold annually, making Sweden the number one nation in this respect.

Banks and post offices

Swedish banks have not gone as far as to charge you an entrance fee - yet. But the days of changing your currency at the bank are gone. Usually bank tellers recommend you to go to Forex.

The yellow and blue post offices ceased to exist in 2002. Today you have to look for their replacement that comes in a somewhat smaller shape. They are located in department stores or shops,

Bananas are popular in Sweden, but we advice against using them as gifts.

where they are well hidden. You simply have to ask the locals to assist you. This is a good exercise to get acquainted with them.

Bathrooms

In Swedish homes they are generally spotless. Often you may choose to use more or less water when you flush by pressing the smaller or larger button. The bathtub has in most cases been replaced with a shower cabin or wall. In quite a few houses the bubble bath (hot tub) has taken over.

Swedes are much more straightforward than many foreign tourists when it comes to the toilet. They may very well exclaim "I must have eaten something my stomach can't handle" or something else to that effect. There is no beating about the bush, unless you are strangers to each other, which you mostly are.

Beauty

Natural beauty comes first in Sweden. To have an operation to improve your looks is a growing trend, much more common than in the early days of the 21st century, but is not out of proportion yet.

Still, among all generations of Swedish women, breasts seem to be a concern. This means breast enlargements are on the increase and leading to a buoyant bra market. Face-lifts also occur. A new phenomenon is to change your upper lip, to fold it upward. Botox and lips seem to be a new popular combination.

The extent of such surgical methods, though, is far from what happens in America. Swedish girls still tend to prefer natural beauty without too much make-up. Training, work-outs and other ways of torturing their bodies are popular. Football, handball, skiing and other sports contribute to their well-being too. This moderate approach goes for clothes as well. They may be expensive but discreet. You want to be seen but not pointed at.

Rumor has it that American TV companies once refused to show British series because the actors and actresses are not handsome or beautiful enough. This makes Swedes laugh. Natural beauty again!

Beggars

For donkey's years there were no beggars in Sweden. Now they are back, this time Romanian and Bulgarian citizens mainly, preferably Roma women and men, who within the framework of the EU have the right to travel freely within the union.

That is why you see beggars sitting outside supermarkets, even in isolated places and on islands. This has stirred the blood of many

Swedes and has led to the division of two groups: those who give money and those who don't. The givers do it for humanitarian reasons, the non-givers for political reasons.

The native countries of the beggars are part of funding programs from the EU and should solve their problems, i.e. to give the Roma a decent life situation. The existence of poor people has once again shown that Sweden is part of something much bigger - the world.

Bergman, Ingmar

Ingmar Bergman (1918-2007), the renowned film director, writer and producer, has been considered one of the greatest names in film in the 20th century. He covered themes like death, illness, faith, sexuality, betrayal, religion, childhood and insanity.

His home on Fårö, an island in the Baltic with a ferry to the Isle of Gotland, plays an important role today. Inhabitants used to direct visitors in the wrong direction to preserve Ingmar Bergman's privacy when he was alive. Even after his death he is still the most famous and controversial Swedish filmmaker. In any case, people come to the small cinema there to watch his films. He is not related to Ingrid Bergman, the Swedish born Hollywood star.

Bergvärme (thermal heating)

The idea of warming your house by getting heat from deep below grew stronger as oil prices went up in the early days of this millennium. Drilling a hole 500 feet deep is quite common in many places. It also reduces the cost of heating as much as 40 percent. The writer of this book has a hole in his garden which is almost 150 meters (164 yards) deep.

Berries and mushrooms

Before the Swedes start shooting elk (moose) in the autumn, they scare off the animals by flocking by the thousands into the forests.

The first wave of people, equipped with buckets and heavy backpacks, goes for two things: berries (raspberries, blueberries, cloudberries or lingonberries) and a picnic (a nice cup of strong coffee from their thermoses and a heap of cheese sandwiches). Foreign pickers from such places as Thailand (6000 of them in 2019) come to make some money by combing the woods for berries. Due to swindlers who have not kept their promises, Asian pickers and others have had to seek financial support to fly back home because they made no profit at all.

The second wave swarming the forests has one beautiful picture in mind: to see a few square feet covered with mushrooms. Big yellow ones with their hats remain the pickers' greatest dream—and for experienced Swedes, this dream will frequently come true. Not only will they fill their baskets with chanterelles but they will also risk their health and lives by picking mushrooms that threaten to lead to renal failure.

Birds

"Swedish birds are blonde." (No jokes about beautiful Swedish tits here!) Apart from that you may find pigeons, sparrows, blackbirds, magpies and jackdaws in any town you visit.

Canada geese are considered a plague all over the country. Better liked are other members of that family, like swans and ducks. Eiders, seagulls, terns and a lot of other sea birds can be seen—and heard—along the coasts. They are part of the summer and belong there. Among the predators, eagles, falcons, hawks and owls dominate. Some of the species can be seen resting on fences along the highways.

"What's that little funny bird called?" an American guest once asked. The answer was: "It's a wagtail" (in Swedish sädesärla). This little grey and black bird with its long, wagging tail spends its summers in Sweden. Like millions of other migratory birds it flies south in the autumn.

Blekinge

For more than 550 years, until 1658, this province in the southeast was part of Denmark. Its beautiful archipelago can be reached from Blekinge's capital, Karlskrona, as well as Hanö, an island in the Baltic, easily visited by boat. For salmon fishing, Mörrumsån (a river) is ideal.

The town Karlskrona in Blekinge, with its large square, was once intended to be the capital of Sweden in case of war. Immigration to America, an important feature of the 19th century, often began in Karlshamn, a picturesque little coastal town. Ronneby, with the old part Bergslagen and a museum, offers historic sites. Sölvesborg, which dates back to medieval days, has got the beautiful St. Nicolai Church.

Blonds

A minority of Swedes are blond, including those who have dyed their hair. If scientists' calculations turn out to be true, there will be no naturally blond people within 200 years. Just in case, come now and see all the blonds, even though the scientists might be wrong.

Boasting

Until the mid-1990s, boasting was frowned upon as a means of personal PR. A professor of nuclear physics would say, "Well, I've got a grasp of physics, but there are certainly others who know more than I do."

The American influence on Swedish life changed this. All of a sudden, Swedish rock groups started behaving as if they were from another planet. "We are the greatest contribution to mankind since the Beatles and Elvis." And followers of this attitude have grown big. The sign "No boasting" has been removed from Sweden Ltd. However, generally speaking Swedes do not tend to brag. This book is a simple attempt to inform and amuse, although it is probably of very low value. See what I mean?

Bohuslän

The province of Bohuslän is situated on the west coast, and ranges from Göteborg (Gothenburg) in the south to the Norwegian border in the north. This ragged, rocky and rural part of Sweden attracts tourists from all over the country. With hundreds of islands, it has many beautiful stops, if you feel like a bit of sailing or fancy renting a summer cottage.

The days of its old fishing villages are gone, and nowadays wealthy Stockholmers and Gothenburgers purchase property on the water's edge. The beautiful bridges, leading to the Isle of Tjörn, are spectacular. So are the rock carvings in Tanumshede. The town of Marstrand, with the old fortress overlooking the island, is idyllic with raw beauty and expensive boats.

Kosteröarna, Sweden's westernmost islands, can be reached by boat from Strömstad, which is a lax paradise for Norwegian guests. Lysekil, a town with a marina and smooth red rocks is a must. Smögen, the most well-known remaining fishing village in Bohuslän, has supposedly got the best prawns in the country. It is not far from Nordens Ark, a zoo aiming to help and breed endangered species.

Boring Swedes

Swedes are dull, foreigners may claim, but I'd say it is not true. They are large, round yellow-fleshed roots which are eaten as vegetables. You could also say that Swedes are friendly people interested in foreigners, especially if they get a chance to speak English. Most Swedes are pretty good at it but a lot are not as advanced as they may think. They still sound Swedish, even when using English words. Tourists say in interviews on television that we are laid back and easy to get along with. The charming Danish, though, probably still argue that we are boring.

Boys and girls

Girls can be friends with boys and boys with girls. This fact can sometimes be hard to explain to foreign guests, or to new Swedes. "We're just friends!" is a common phrase. A girl can sit on a boy's lap or she can massage his back—and they're still only friends. These sexless relationships surprise visitors. After breaking up, a couple may say, "We're still good friends!" Dear reader, go on, ask young people about it!

Boring Swedes?

Breakfast

If you spell this word "brakfest," it would mean "hell of a party" in Swedish. That has nothing to do with a proper Swedish breakfast. Do not expect jam, marmalade or peanut butter on your bread. The odds are far better that you will be served cheese, ham or spread cheese for breakfast. They may add green and red pepper, cucumber or slices of tomato to their morning meal. Orange juice and cereals are often served in hotels and guest houses. Swedes tend to find sweet, sticky breakfasts disgustingly unhealthy, so they save up all their sweet and sticky buns for later in the day when the nation sits down for coffee.

Breastfeeding

Swedish mothers tend to breastfeed their children much more and much longer than mothers in countries like the USA. It is supposed to give the child a better start in life, physically and mentally. It is quite common in public places as well.

Mothers give birth to 115,000-120,000 babies each year here, which puts the country in one of the leading positions in Europe as far as birth rates are concerned. Ethnic minorities probably contribute to the high number of babies, like they do in many Western countries.

Business meetings

At a regular business meeting the foreign participant will notice that a Swedish executive or managing director is more of a team member than a god. This person may not even sit at the end of the table. He or she expects staff members to express their opinions and they will get all the attention they need. It may seem time consuming. Still, that is often the way negotiations are conducted. Even after a "yes" to the deal, discussions may continue.

The coffee break might come as a surprise but plays an essential part in Sweden. It cannot be postponed or cancelled, as all Swedes will get symptoms like headaches, which isn't good for business. (See Fika!)

When the time has come to celebrate the agreement, do not expect to spend the evening in a bar or on the town. This is out of the question, especially if the Swedish party is a state owned company, local authority or public television. The word "scandal" would be written all over the media as soon as they got wind of it.

Candy

Like so many others, Swedes have a sweet tooth. Every supermarket has a section pick n' mix (plockgodis) where you may choose the sweets you prefer and put them in a small paper bag. In some shops the assortment differs in size, but mainly the same kind of candy can be found in any department store or other food shop.

The habit of taking your children to buy candy on Saturday afternoon lingers on. "Saturday Candy Express" returns home with happy kids who are supposed to leave their sweets untouched until the evening—with their favorite TV program. For some children, sweets can be eaten only on Saturday. Extra pocket money, used as blackmail, may be saved for something more useful.

Swedes consume more sweets than any nationality in the world (2017), except for the Danes, our happy sweet tooth neighbors. Statistics change all the time.

Cars

Now that Rolls Royce has German owners, Swedes do not have to be sad about Volvo Cars being a Chinese company. Volvo Group, the producer of trucks, still resides in Göteborg but with big Chinese share owners.

As for Saab, that is another sad, never ending story. Scania, Volvo Group's major competitor in trucks, now flies the German flag, but things change faster than you can say second gear.

The best-selling Swedish car in all categories, Ahlgrens Bilar, still holds their peak position. It's got a nice flavor, needs no maintenance and is eaten a lot.

Cashless Sweden

Sweden is rapidly going cashless. You cannot always use cash to pay at a café, a shop, a parking meter or for transportation. Apps are frequently used instead. A popular way of transferring money is to use Swish, a simple way to pay privately or publicly. Sweden's national bank, Riksbanken, is already preparing its own cryptocurrency in the form of digital kronor.

Celebrities

There are two categories of celebrities in Sweden. The first one contains Nobel Prize winners, scientists, authors, painters and dancers. Names like Arvid Carlsson, Selma Lagerlöf, Nils Dardel and Malin Ek belong here. A criterion to qualify for this category is that no one, not even every Swede, has ever heard of them.

In the second category, film stars, pop- and rock stars, tennis players and football coaches gather. Ingrid Bergman, Greta Garbo, Abba, Roxette, Björn Borg, Zlatan Ibrahimovic and soccer coach Sven Göran Ericsson are part of this Hall of Fame. In this case, everyone has heard of them. Raoul Wallenberg, who saved tens of thousands of Jews during the last months of World War II, and Dag Hammarskjöld, the UN general secretary killed in a plane crash in the Congo, most likely belong to this group.

The first rule of being a celebrity, be it a pop star, an actress or a member of the government is to be "the man or woman next door." He or she does not drive a flashy car but invests money so nobody will get the impression that they are showing off. Political leaders may be expected to cut up salmon on a TV-talk show, wade to their knees in water in their new suits, answer questions about their sex life and get insulted by getting childish questions—all this to show that they are "ordinary" people. Stars go to the local store to buy their necessities.

Cell phones (mobile phones)

Regardless of age, sex, ethnic group or profession, Swedes use mobile phones everywhere. Expect to see children sending text messages or older teenagers talking about life's important phases, retired people making short calls and everyone else talking nonsense.

Each member of a family often has their own mobile phone. Swedes have a special relationship to their little electronic devices, like so many people around the world today. There are even mobile-free zones on trains these days, a step taken by the railway companies because of the terror of mobile flashers who speak in loud voices about very private matters, discussing flings with their wives or the neighbor's high salary. When Swedes go to America they have to make sure their phones are working there.

Bear in mind that there are many wi-fi spots in shops, hotels, libraries and other places in Sweden that are free of charge. So, please check your own mobile phone before leaving for Sweden to avoid any kind of practical problem. By the way, if you rent an automobile you are not allowed to use your cell phone while driving, unless it is hands-free.

Cemeteries

"Our cemetery in Jesmond Road looks like it has been left to its own fate, but here they are so well kept," said a man from Newcastle, England, who was studying the graves in Lerum, a small town east of Gothenburg. He explained that he found everything so neat and perfect, as if someone was looking after the churchyard and every single grave on a daily basis.

The fact is that employees at local cemeteries are paid to do the job. Due to migration within the country, lots of families have no one to attend to their family graves otherwise. If graves are left in poor condition, the next-of-kin will receive a letter or find a message at the grave explaining that they will have to make sure it is in good order or it will be dug up and used for someone else. Big ads in newspapers may contain a warning, that unless something is done about a grave, immediate steps will be taken in this direction. Once again the Swedish sense of order reigns.

Why not take a look at a cemetery while there? And be thankful you are not one of the residents.

Children

The silent child at a party or family reunion, the one who anxiously looks at a parent to make sure it is OK to speak, hardly exists in Sweden. Children are encouraged to take part in conversations in most modern families. Foreign guests have been known to express their irritation for spoiled Swedish brats.

To see this eagerness as a result of bad upbringing is to misun-

Children in Sweden are known to express their opinions freely.

derstand the whole situation. A Swede would ask: Why not allow children to express their opinions? This is, after all, the best training in natural situations and enables children to grow up mentally and develop their personality.

Children's names

The frequency of various names will change all the time. The following names were very popular at the time of this book being published. For girls: Elsa, Alice, Maja, Agnes, Lilly, Olivia, Julia, Ebba, Linnea, Molly. For boys: William, Lucas, Liam, Oscar, Elias, Hugo, Oliver, Charlie, Axel, Vincent.

At #43 Mohamad's name comes up, a sign of a changing Sweden. The observant reader will notice that the Anglo-Saxon world and Sweden have a lot in common with regard to children's names.

Christmas

As in so many other countries, streets and department stores are illuminated and decorated from early November onward. The goal is to open people's eyes toward the most important festival of the year—Christmas—which is surpassed by no other celebration during a normal year.

The important day in Sweden is Christmas Eve on December 24. Each family naturally has developed its own customs and traditions, but some traits seem to be of a common nature. Christmas Eve might look like the following standard model:

The tree has been lit up and presents put underneath it. On the morning of Christmas Eve day, ham forms part of a minor smörgåsbord. Special non-alcoholic beverages like "julmust" (sweet, brown soda in bottles) are served. Then the suffering part follows. Children have to wait for grandmother and grandfather to arrive—or go to their home instead. This inactive period finishes in the afternoon. "Glögg" (hot, alcoholic drink with raisins and almonds) is served. At 3 p.m. the Disney parade on television commences. It consists of excerpts from well-known stories with Donald Duck, Robin Hood and Cinderella, just to mention a few. Traditionally millions of Swedes spend this hour watching TV.

Then a large smörgåsbord is served in many homes. By the time you feel sleepy from eating herring, salmon, ham, sausages and meatballs, the jolly old tomte in red may be spotted outside. When the young members of the family have lost pieces of their new toys and all the male members have failed to get some electronic device going, coffee is served and fruit and soft drinks appear. At midnight when all adults have collapsed in their armchairs the little ones carry on playing with their Christmas gifts.

On December 25, fathers and mothers promise to buy fewer presents next Christmas, exactly what they promised the previous year. This day used to be a boring day, when restaurants and bars were closed. Nowadays the youth often spend this evening with friends.

Swedes often invite or are invited to friends on Boxing Day, the second day of Christmas (Annandag jul). In an attempt to get away from the smörgåsbord, Swedes have copied the British-American tradition of eating turkey.

The tradition of julgransplundring, "plundering the Christmas tree," a party to please the children, has died out in most homes. The idea was to finish celebrations in early January by stripping the Christmas tree of its lights, flags and other decorations, and then chuck it out the window.

Approximately 500,000 of the ten million inhabitants do not celebrate Christmas for religious reasons. Sweden's Muslim community has expanded slowly but dramatically over the last decades and probably makes up the largest ethnic group. An estimated number varies from 800,000 to one million, but these are not official figures. Take them with a grain of salt.

Climate

Swedes tend to exaggerate when describing their homeland with cold days, blizzards and tons of snow covering their homes. In Småland's highlands in central Sweden and in the north the description may fit, but the worst performers are the Swedish subjects from the south, where weather is generally temperate, even in the winter.

In a good year, summers can compare favorably to the Mediterranean area with hot, sunny days and warm water for swimming. In a bad year you will face rain, wind, sunshine, heat, rain again, clouds, rain and sunshine, and more rain.

Coffee

The Swedes love their coffee. With or without cream it will be drunk in factories, offices, schools, public buildings and hospitals, not only once a day or even twice but maybe four or five times. The less important your job is the more coffee you drink. Try and ask people how much coffee they gulp a day!

To a visitor, Swedish coffee may appear too strong but that's the way the Swedes want it. Over the years, espresso, Americano, caffé macchiato, cappuccino and other names have sneaked into Swedish cafés and coffee shops. They are now part of the nation's taste in coffee.

Conservatories (sunrooms)

A conservatory is a glass-enclosed portion of a home used as a sunroom or a three-season lounge. The Swedes often refer to it as a senior citizen incubator. You see, old people are always treated with respect. The number of these outdoor rooms has increased countrywide and is considered a normal part of housing today.

Costumes

Old peasant costumes (folkdräkter) may no longer seem to belong in the modern world. Still, at Christmas, Easter and Midsummer, and at weddings, christenings and other special occasions, they emerge from closets all over the country in restricted numbers.

Strict rules regulate the material used and the way the costumes look. Each part of the country, even smaller than a province/county, has got its own costume. Most Swedes probably connect this habit with Dalarna, Lappland and Småland just to mention a few provinces.

Crayfish parties

When summer days get shorter and vacations are over, the Swedes need a reason for having a good time, i.e. a crayfish party (kräftskiva). If you should accidentally be in Sweden in early August and hear people singing outdoors, the reason may well be a "kräftskiva."

Take a closer look and you will see a party of people wearing silly hats and sitting at a table, eating crayfish, cracking claws, sucking at crayfish heads and singing songs and drinking schnapps in between. Look around and you will notice illuminated decorations like moons and suns in bushes and on porches.

In some parts of the country you catch your own crayfish at night in the local brook or river, starting in early August.

Like so many other traditions, crayfish parties face the danger of dying out in the future. Young Swedes do not tend to take part in these activities the way older people do. Crayfish suck or people suck crayfish.

Dagens (lunch)

All over the country you will see the sign "Dagens rätt" (Today´s dish) or "Dagens lunch" (Today´s lunch). It is usually situated outside restaurants around lunchtime, except for Saturdays and Sundays. The meaning of the words is simply "dish of the day," and could be said to be something like "affordable lunch". You may have a choice of three dishes at least. The price usually includes a salad buffet, bread and butter, and water as well as coffee, possibly with a biscuit. In 2019 you could get a good lunch at about 100 Swedish kronor, give or take ten kronor. God aptit. (Add an o in the first word and pe plus e in the second one and you will get the message.)

Dagny

Dagny Carlsson, this famous and probably oldest blogger (Bojan) in the world was born in 1912 and at the age of 107 she was still active. When she was 99 years she attended a computer course, which in its turn led the establishment of her own courses for retired people. Her formula for a long, successful life is simply "good genes and curiosity". She has fans from Japan to Europe. Dagny has appeared on television a lot and has been introduced to the Swedish royal family and celebrities of all kinds.

Dalarna

This is the number one "Swedish" province, in close competition with Gotland. Folk music, the red wooden horses (Dalahästar), skiing and mines are all part of the image of Dalarna. Lake Siljan, Sweden's seventh largest lake, is the wheel around which everything revolves. The Isle of Sollerön with its roots in prehistoric days has a large number of graves.

Some exhibits are displayed in Dalarna's Museum in Falun, a town where the Falu Coppermine invites you to see the interior of the old mine. It was in use for more than 700 years and is where the famous red color used for painting farms and houses saw the light and lasted well into the 20th century. Gesunda mountain, south of Mora, gives the visitor a spectacular view from its peak. At the base of the mountain you will find Tomtelandet, Father Christmas's dwelling. For nature lovers, Hamra National Park lies north of Orsa.

Husbyringen is a 35-mile road that takes you to mansions and former industries. It is strongly recommended. So are Storstupet and Styggforsen, two waterfalls in Dalarna.

The estates once belonging to Carl Larsson and Anders Zorn, two of Sweden's best known painters, are open to the public (in Sundborn and in Mora). So is the annual cross-country ski competition Vasaloppet (with 15,000 competitors), which takes place in early March and is some 56 miles in length. Sälen in the north is the starting point of Vasaloppet, a winter resort that also offers downhill skiing. Nittsjö with its pottery is open every day of the week.

Towns to be visited are Avesta with its coin museum and Gamla Byn (old houses), Hedemora, the oldest town in the province, Ludvika with modern industries and Mine Museum, and Borlänge with its collection of minerals in the Geological Museum.

Dalsland

The province of Dalsland, a Sweden in miniature, has green forests and blue lakes (more water than in any other province actually). It offers lots of activities for lovers of the outdoors. Dalsland's Canal (160 miles of waterway) with the famous aqueduct at Håverud, connects lakes through a network of rivers and brooks, all a real paradise for active tourists.

Åmål, dating from 1643, is the only town here. In the 1998 Lukas Moodysson film "Fucking Åmål" (in English Show Me Love), the truth, i.e. how boring teenage life can be, came out in the open.

Deadlines

Deadlines exist because they look proper and suitable. For the pragmatic Swede this does not constitute a problem. They are dead before they are even lines. There are ways to avoid that tricky date. The most common approach is to set a new date, and possibly another one.

This is due to the fact that the ordinary Swede has been trained to "understand" other fellow citizens, to demonstrate empathy and to reach a consensus. Maybe the library book was not handed in on time because of heavy rain. If you do not hand in your tax declaration on time though, you might face a fine, but not necessarily.

Decisions (Beslut)

They are made albeit most of the time by reaching a consensus. Most organizations and corporations are run in an egalitarian way where the man or woman in charge is seen as a team leader rather than the final decision maker. It is like a scene from a comedy video where a Swedish army truck full of soldiers can´t fire their guns before everyone has had time to give their opinion on the current situation.

Delaware

Settlers arrived in 1609, and between the years 1638–1655 the state was a Swedish colony. It included parts of Pennsylvania and New Jersey. Then the Dutch, the English and finally the Americans took over.

Did you know this about Sweden?

- There are wild orchids.
- Walnuts grow in certain places and are cultivated.
- Wine is made from domestic grapes.

- Tropical summer nights are not uncommon.
- As a result of the inland ice the country is still rising. Part of the coastline has risen 300 meters the last 10,000 years.
- Andersson is the most common family name. An average family has 1.55 children (!).
- Being a sambo means to live family life without being married. A mambo still lives with mom and a bamboo is a plant used for decoration.

Dial-a-Swede

The Swedish Tourist Association, Visit Sweden, created the "Swedish number." The idea was to connect the international caller to a random Swede. The contact would hopefully lead to a conversation about anything. And believe it or not, the USA attracted most calls. The number is no longer in use and, please don't dial mine.

Disabled, the

Improvements in enabling good lives for disabled people have been made throughout society. Any disabled child or adult would probably disagree. We still have a long way to go before we reach perfection.

Pavement is constructed to enable wheelchairs to wheel on and off. Public toilets usually have one stall with a wide door and special equipment to ensure that a wheelchair can get in and out. Public buildings, such as town halls, must have ramps to provide wheelchair access. "Call-a-bus" services operate in villages, towns and cities so that disabled citizens can get to a doctor or see a friend or relative. Strict and concerning requirements for all new buildings, even private, are in operation in "boy-does-that-sound-perfect-land" to facilitate life for the disabled.

Discussions

Heated discussions between shop assistants and customers, motorists on the road, colleagues or friends are far less frequent than in more fiery countries where people show their feelings. They are usually settled through arguments either pro- or con- the cause of the argument. Swedes will often get "lagom" upset when tourists tell off a waiter or treat them badly. On the whole the atmosphere seems calm on the surface in a Swedish discussion.

This cool attitude may best be described by going back to an interview after the Estonia disaster, where more than 850 lives were lost in a ferry accident. A Swedish man was waiting for news about whether his son had survived. When French television asked him questions, he remained calm, something the reporter said would never have happened in his country. The next-of-kin would have been weeping and sobbing or paralyzed by grief and anxiety. He told them he had been there for hours. There was still hope. Luckily his son had survived.

DNA

The ordinary ethnic Swede, or the new Swede, has no clue what haplogroup they belong to. And why should they? This is new science and knowledge.

A haplogroup is a people, a tribe or group with the same genetic background. Swedes generally belong to R1a, R1b or to haplogroup I, the largest one. Those with Finnish background may belong to N instead. Immigrants from Turkey could be J1 and J2, people from Iran, Iraq and Kurdish Iraq possibly J too. In India, H and R1a are common. The number taking tests increases by the day. In 2018 about 70,000 Swedes had found out about their ancestry.

Doors

The Doors still have a following in Sweden after all these rock 'n' roll years. Swedish toilet doors on the other hand—or any door for that matter—may be a problem among English-speaking guests. Why? In fact, you open a toilet door by pulling it toward you. When leaving you push the door away from you. Also, a closed rest room door doesn't automatically mean it's occupied.

Most Swedish doors look solid, and often the entrance has one outer and one inner door. In the north you will find entrance doors with mosquito nets plus glass. It will save you from getting dozens of these blood-drinking mini-Draculas all over you.

In parts of rural Sweden residents will leave their front doors open. This open-door policy means that suddenly a neighbor may enter your kitchen, saying "hello." For safety reasons no information can be given away to foreign tourists where this habit still lives on (a joke!).

Drink and drive

"Who is driving?" This very common question will be heard at every party before the first drink or glass of wine is poured. The loser, i.e. the person who will drive home from the party, has to stick to light beer or non-alcoholic beverages.

The laws are strict and "no" alcohol (officially maximum 0.2 blood alcohol level) is allowed in a driver. Breathalyzers are in use to keep the Swedes in line. There is a shortage of police officers, so you may get away. That is the good news. The bad news is that it is totally wrong. Drinking and driving do not make a perfect match.

Drugstores

Got a cold? Look for the Apotek sign, which is displayed in or around every square of every one-horse town.

If you have a prescription, go to Recept, or if you require an ordinary aspirin or bandage, go to the counter not marked Recept or to the desk. The word "recept" means recipe and prescription in Swedish.

Easter

In parts of the country bonfires are lit on the day before Easter. Little girls dress like witches (häxor) and little boys put on hats and mustaches. They often knock on neighbors' doors to offer homemade cards in exchange for a coin or possibly some candy. They do not shout "trick or treat" though.

Crackers, rockets and other kinds of fireworks roar into the sky while dogs hide under beds and behind sofas. Due to accidents and damaged ears, the loud sound bit is now being down played. The fact that dogs suffer from loud sounds has contributed to decreasing sales of noisy products.

Between Christmas and Easter "semlor" are eaten. These buns, containing marzipan and whipped cream, should traditionally be eaten in hot milk with cinnamon all over, a tradition on its way to the history dump. Most people eat it like a bun, getting whipped cream all over their faces.

Eating

It is carried out in the same way as in the US or Canada, i.e. with your mouth. Mind you, Swedes hold the fork in their left hand and the knife in their right hand. The habit of using your fork only has established itself due to American films, but is not considered the appropriate way by many a Swede of a certain age. You do not generally peal an apple or similar fruit. Bananas are an exception. They are, on the other hand, botanically a berry.

Economy

You might describe Swedish economy as a combination of a capitalist system and a great influence by the state.

Privately owned companies account for a vast majority of industrial activities. ABB, SKF, Volvo, Scania (trucks), Ericsson, Hessle (medical products and research) and Stora (timber) are names of large enterprises. Agriculture today plays a somewhat obscure role and products such as vegetables and fruits are often imported.

Exports go to Germany, other EU-nations, the UK, USA and Norway. They include machinery, cars, paper products, iron and steel and popular music. Imports include oil and petrol, chemicals, food, clothing and electronic goods, among others.

The country claims to have "one of the lowest levels of national debt, low and stable inflation in the EU and a healthy banking system" (source: Sweden Sverige).

Great investments have been made in healthcare, education and research. In 2018 the export of vehicles and machines dominated. Surprisingly, taxes have been lowered since the crisis in the 1990s.

Edible Country

This is a new project by Visit Sweden that transforms all of Sweden into an outdoor gourmet restaurant. People can choose from menus co-created by four of Sweden's top chefs, book a picnic table (at www.visitsweden.com or www.bookatable.com) in one of 13 remote locations, then forage and cook their own food. Recipes along with information on how to properly cook the multi-course menus are available online and a cooking kit containing the necessary tools as well as a personal guide or chef along with a basket of ingredients can be booked at an additional cost. In order to avoid the loss of lives participants are not allowed to pick their own mushrooms (including the fly agaric or death cap eaten by the Vikings to get high, but mostly resulting in them getting very low, in fact 6 feet under).

Electricity

People in Sweden spend a lot of money on electricity. That is part of their lifestyle. 220 volts come through wall sockets with only two holes. You will have to buy an adapter to use your electric shaver, hairdryer or Powerbook. In 2002, after a dry summer and a cold winter, prices doubled, but that did not change people's habits. They simply complained. In 2015 the situation was much more favorable for consumers—and people did not complain.

Electronics

Swedes have a soft spot for electronic gadgets, such as computers, tablets and smartphones. 60,000 teachers nationwide were each given (under certain conditions) a computer after attending a long training course. This was government policy in an attempt to promote the use of computers in schools in the early 21st century.

Senior citizens form internet clubs, where more advanced users of this medium assist other retired people. In 2019 the oldest blogger, Dagny Carlsson, celebrated her 107th birthday.

Even the young ones are involved in this new world. One 4-year-old girl explained how to use the family computer by telling her aunt: "First you climb up on the table, where the computer is. Then you switch it on at the back...." This took place before the days of the laptops.

Edible country? All of Sweden can be served on a plate, albeit not literally.

Emigration

In the early to mid 1800s the first wave of immigration to the United States of America got under way. In 1846 a religious cult set out and founded Bishop Hills, Illinois.

A few decades later the number of ships sailing across the Atlantic to the big country in the west increased rapidly. Emigrants continued to cross the huge ocean in search of prosperity and a piece of land of their own. Over one million Swedes (probably close to 1.3 million) left their homeland due to famine and failing crops and this emigration continued well into the 20th century.

Generally they arrived in New York. Though thousands stayed there, many moved to the states around the Great Lakes, like Minnesota and Illinois. The numbers amounted to hundreds of thousands, either Swedish families or male individuals.

At one time Chicago had such a large Swedish population, that it was only outnumbered by Stockholm. This great influx of Swedish immigrants led to the founding of towns like Stockholm, Gothenburg, Lindsborg, Lindstrom and Vasa. An estimated number of eight million Americans are said to have Swedish blood. Other sources claim over 10 million. The writer of this book has family in several US states.

Equality

Swedes are very proud of their sense of equality. Gone are the days of making jokes about housewives not leaving the kitchen or showing your homophobia by cracking silly jokes. You will be smiled at in an awkward way, which could best be translated as "you silly foreign fart, you think you're funny, eh?" Refrain from ethnically based jokes. You are not in New York—no Jewish jokes, please. That would be a torable shame!

In Swedish schools there isn't a teachers' break room. Instead there is one staff room, which invites anybody from the principal to the janitor to drink coffee or have a chat.

The government has an expressed wish to make certain half of all ministers and MPs are female (2018: 54% men, 46% women). This is to make it easy and practical on the last day of parliament before summer at the evening dance. The same rules apply as at other dances: Ladies are allowed to ask men to dance. The more wine they drink, the more common it gets.

As far as male and female salaries are concerned, the rule of equality does not quite apply. In fact the gap in some cases widens. "But we are working on it," as politicians say.

Swedes started to travel early. The emigrant waves of the 19th century came later.

EU

Sweden's entry into the European Union took place in 1995 in an election where 52.2% of the voters were for it and 46.9% against. The introduction of the euro never happened so our currency is still the Swedish krona. The division in this vital issue cut straight through the political parties. The overall opinion today is pro-EU.

Eurovision Song Contest

The extensive competition where far more than 40 European countries compete about the best song of the year has really gone down well among Swedes. The preliminary domestic competition, where 32 songs are reduced to one in the Swedish leg of the show, has a large following.

Sweden has been one of the most successful nations, winning five times so far, which almost puts the country in the same league as Ireland. Since the fall of the Iron Wall, Eastern European countries have proven themselves worthy of participation by scoring good results. To some countries it is merely a competition, to the Swedes it's a craze that keeps the nation in excitement for weeks. Swedish songwriting teams even write contributions for a number of countries. Each year journalists claim the "songs are worse than ever and the artists terrible." Still, it is the most watched TV show every year.

Exchange students

A Swedish exchange student arriving in America will be the center of attention at a college and will be invited to parties by everyone. This euphoria will cease after two weeks though, and everyone will forget about them, according to unreliable young Swedes who have been there.

In Sweden, however, an exchange student might initially be lonely, unless he meets other students right away and asks questions about the teachers, everyday life and school. After a while, which in this case means weeks or even months, the exchange student will love them, and by the time of departure the process of leaving will be hard. There will be tears, hugs, an exchange of contact information and "see you soon." Swedes tend to be slow at first, but loyal later on.

Remember that most classes are already shaped and friendships between various students have developed by the time the newcomer arrives. It might be tricky to fit in. What seems like disinterest is simply insecurity. It has nothing to do with the fact that the newcomer is a foreigner. Try to fit in anyway, and there will always be the kind students who look after the new friend.

As for the meals that are served in schools, you may choose between ordinary food, vegetarian and/or vegan food in many cases. And, read this twice: It is absolutely free of charge. Bon appétit.

When you are full, you realize the language problem exists, although it may seem as if everybody understands English well. The Swedish students are the underdogs linguistically. Keep up your good sense of humor and you will experience a pleasant year in Sweden! And be like German and Swiss exchange students: Learn Swedish as soon as possible. Go for it.

Expressions

Let's compare Swedish and English sayings and expressions. Swedish expressions first in translation word for word.

- Burned child shuns the fire = Once bitten, twice shy
- Walk like the cat around hot porridge = Beat around the bush
- No danger on the roof = No worries
- Dressed up to their teeth = Dressed to the nines
- Not having clean flour in your bag = Having a skeleton in your closet
- There is a dog buried here = There is something fishy going on
- I sense owls in the bog = Something's wrong, let's work it out

- Give back for old cheese = Seek revenge
- Hold your thumbs = Keep your fingers crossed
- Hit two flies with one slap = Kill two birds with one stone
- Make a hen out of a feather = Make a mountain out of a molehill
- Away is fine but home is best = Home is where the heart is
- This Svensson book is great = Nonsense

Facts and figures - The Very Official Guide to the Swedes

The Kingdom of Sweden: The country won its independence from Denmark and soon after, on June 6, 1523, Gustav Vasa was elected king. This is a national holiday nowadays.

- Flag: blue with a yellow cross, one of the oldest flags in the world
- Total area: 173,732 square miles (land: 158,662 square miles)
- Highest point: Mt Kebnekaise: 6,909 feet, still melting
- Number of lakes: a little less than 100,000
- Population: 10,272,518 (May 2019)
- Biggest cities: Stockholm 750,000 (Greater Stockholm 1,560,000), Gothenburg (Göteborg) 470,000 (Greater Gothenburg 590,000), Malmö 312,000.
- Natural resources: ore, timber, hydropower
- Life expectancy: women 84.1 years, men 80.6 years in 2018 (higher than the UK and the United States)
- Religions (approximate numbers, unreliable facts): Lutherans appr. 67%, Muslims 5%, Catholics 2% (110,000), Pentecostals 106,000 members, Orthodox groups 120,000, plus Baptists and other churches

- Administrative divisions: 21 counties or provinces (län); in this book 25, according to the earlier division of landskap. Norrland covers 58% of the area but with only 13% of the population.
- Parliament: Social Democrats, the Moderates, the Left Party (includes socialists and former communists), the Christian Democrats, the Centre Party (formerly with a majority in the countryside, now also urban), the Liberal Party, the Green Party, and the Sweden Democrats (for which immigration is the big issue). Representatives are elected on four-year terms. A party receiving less than 4.0% of the votes will get no representation.

Historically, the Social Democrats were the largest party for decades with 35–45% of the votes, and in the odd election even more. Today the percentage is much lower. The Social Democrats, the Left Party and the Green Party form a block in Parliament that generally beats the Liberal Party, the Center Party, the Christian Democrats and the outsider the Sweden Democrats. In recent elections both sides have alternatively formed governments. In 2018 it was a complicated draw between the two sides and the Sweden Democrats getting 17.5%. The result was a government consisting of the Social Democrats and the Green Party, relying on support by the Left Party, the Liberals and the Center Party.

Fake news

"Last night in Sweden ..." President Trump talked about violence in Sweden but had not checked the facts. The nation was as peaceful as ever, also that night. Riots occurring in the suburbs all the time is another piece of fake news. Of course not. When they happen they are big news, but how often do they take place? Seldom.

Gang rapes are frequent. Well, Afghan boys and youngsters from North Africa have been involved in at least two of these activities, but does that make immigrants rapists? Of course not. We have to check frequency and numbers before jumping to conclusions when it comes to the news. The situation is however complicated.

Family names

You may divide Swedish family names into at least six categories. The "–son names" are the most common. If you endure more than one week's stay in the Monarchy of Sweden, you will undoubtedly come across cheerful Swedes having names like Andersson, Johansson and Pettersson, all with a double s, and in rare cases with only one s or even a z, like Swenzon and Anderzon. The former use of "daughter" as in Andersdaughter (Andersdotter) or Johansdaughter (Johansdotter) is rarely seen in Sweden nowadays. This is the first category.

The second category includes names that deal with nature in one form or another. Mr. Southmountain (Söderberg) may invite Mr. and Mrs. Brookcurrent (Bäckström), or their neighbor Ms. Smallriverrapids (Forsström), to a party at their summerhouse. Other guests may possibly be the Grovetwigs (Lundkvist), the Leafbranches (Lövgren), the Seavalleys (Sjödal) and the Oakwoods (Ekskog). The Bearmountains (Björnberg), the Islemountains (Öberg) and the Birchmen (Björkman) may also receive an invitation.

The third category contains words that have a semi-Latin appearance. In the old days, about 10 generations ago, clergymen did not want to be part of the tradition of adopting their father's first name plus the word son i. e. Johan's son would be Johansson. If this son was called Carl his son would be Carlsson. Instead they chose the village or the town where they lived or came from and gave the name a touch of Latin. That's where names like Amnéus, Burelius, Orstadius and Helsingius have their origin.

The fourth category embraces soldiers' names like Strong, Happy, Well and Beautiful, Branch and Grove.

In the fifth category you will find the nobility, with all their prefixes of von, de and af. In many cases the names are of German origin, others are Scottish or Baltic.

The sixth and last category contains the new Swedes arriving from former Yugoslavia, Turkey, the Middle East, Iran, Afghanistan, South America and Somalia.

Faucets (Taps)

Having one cold-water faucet and one hot water faucet will bring tears to a Swedish tourist abroad. To his or her practical thinking this idea shows how little some nations have developed since the days of Cromwell or Lincoln. What you need is a mixer. The water pours out of the same hole, at the exact temperature of your choice. Thus you can avoid being boiled or getting freezing cold water on the other. That goes for the shower too. One doesn't want to risk one's life, does one?

Feminism

Any politician who does not openly plead allegiance to feminism and equal rights is a dead dinosaur. In most cases it is probably a genuine belief, in others not. There is also a new political party called Feministic Initiative with seats in some towns. So far they have not made it to Parliament.

Ferries

For any tourist who wants to experience a nice crossing on a ferry in Sweden, a feeling of well-being may come across them, as expressed in many a song. There are numerous ferries that take you across straits, rivers and bays. The good news is that most of the yellow ferries are free. The bad news is that some others may charge you a tiny sum. Bridges that have replaced some of the ferries have no tolls. By the way, there are hardly any toll roads in the country. (See Vägtull!)

Fiftieth birthday

Swedes have got this craze about their 50th birthday. At work, in the family, among neighbors, everyone joins in to celebrate.

Such a birthday may well begin about 50 seconds after midnight. If it's outside, there will be cheering, fireworks and uninvited guests carrying plates of food and beverages. They might leave in the early hours so they can come back for more fun later in the afternoon or evening. Neighbors will probably find posters all over the place of the happy face of the 50-year-old sod. Some clever young relatives may also have put a sheet with a message on a wall asking motorists to honk every time they pass the house. But normal celebration also takes place all the time, luckily enough, and that is the common way.

The object of their admiration might rent a restaurant, a club, use their garage—or in the worst case—their own home. Guests can expect a cold buffet, wine, beer, cakes and balloons. The garden will be stripped of branches, twigs and flowers. They will be cut and placed inside the room, where this glorious day is celebrated, if the season allows that, and they live in a house.

And there are songs and speeches, the latter usually quite short because nobody wants to hear that pathetic nonsense. Guests all bring presents like vases, books, more vases, golf clubs, still more vases or an electric lawn mower. A box of whisky or possibly a vase (heard it before?) may be other popular presents.

This unique occasion gives neighbors or colleagues a chance to meet the birthday child's family and vice versa. It will only happen once again, on the victim's 60th birthday. Or, beware, even later on. The writer of this book got birthday presents like a sail boat trip including lunch, a car ride to a spectacular mountain with lunch, restaurant visits and loads of books. In fact, guests may even have met on his or her 30th or 40th birthday, as this craze seems to be afflicting ever younger people. The next thing will probably be behaving in the same way when a child is being born, although toddlers don't usually own garages, so there is a chance they might get out of it.

Even at work surprises may happen. Presents and cakes are possible ways of expressing people's commiserations for the person entering the age of incontinence and menopause. Again, celebrations may be cooled down a bit. Some simply prefer a nice dinner.

Fika

"Let's fika!" "Would you like to fika now?" You can "fika" at work, in town, on your lawn or on a ragged rock. It simply means to drink coffee—and hasn't got a sophisticated ceremony or solemnity about it.

At work you take a break to fika, at home you will fika after meals or after a long walk. On some occasions you can fika and that's it. On others you have something sweet with it, like a cinnamon roll or even a strawberry cake on someone's birthday or just because you want to celebrate summer or because some political party has lost.

Older generations always offered seven kinds of cookies with their fika. It still happens, probably more in the countryside than in towns and cities, but the cookies are slowly fading out. This tradition has gotten lost among the younger generations. But fika itself has strengthened its hold on people through the new coffee shops that seem to replace the traditional konditori, which is a combined bakery and coffee shop. (Don't miss a visit to Vetekatten or Tössebageriet next time you're in Stockholm, and Ahlströms Konditori in Göteborg!)

First lesson of Swedish grammar

boy:	pojke	boys: pojkar
the boy:	pojken	the boys: pojkarna

Notice how the words have different endings.

girl:	flicka	girls: flickor
the girl:	flickan	the girls: flickorna

Notice how the same endings as in boy do not apply. There are at least six ways of forming the plural: pojke-pojkar, flicka-flickor, ärta-ärter, knä-knän, hit-hits, hus- hus

Verbs are fairly simple:

	The present tense	**past imperfect**
I play:	jag spelar	jag spelade
you play:	du spelar	du spelade
he plays:	han spelar	han spelade
she plays:	hon spelar	hon spelade.
it plays:	den/det spelar	det/den spelade
we play:	vi spelar	vi spelade
you play:	ni spelar	ni spelade
they play:	de (dom) spelar	de/dom spelade

Adjectives may have a structure like the following example:

a nice boy: en trevlig pojke

the nice boy: den trevliga pojken

nice boys: trevliga pojkar

the nice boys: de trevliga pojkarna

Fishballs (Fiskbullar)

To any Swede the word "balls" still refers to football (soccer) or tennis, nothing else. We are not like the dirty-minded British, Americans or Australians. The word "fishballs" on the other hand brings to mind unhappy childhood memories (for middle-aged and older people) when you had to eat these balls of minced fish. The only thing that made them edible was the sauce. You can still buy them in tins. Do not attempt to do so!

[The] Swede

Flogsta scream. Screaming is considered good for students. On occasion.

Flags

The Swedish blue flag with a golden-yellow Scandinavian cross flies everywhere on private land. Foreign guests sometimes comment about this. In fact, flags in the gardens or balconies of private homes and properties can be seen all over. In established communities with old houses, the flag inevitably flies in the yard on national holidays, on someone's birthday or on a summer day. It is there to support a clear blue sky or simply to make people feel happy.

When asked what a Swedish 10-year-old girl thought about the colors, she had a suggestion for change: "They should be white as the snow, green as the forests and blue as the lakes." Today, provinces have their own flags to manifest their independence somehow. Even the Church has its own flag.

Flogsta scream, the

In the university town of Uppsala, you may hear the famous "Flogsta scream." Students can be heard screaming, shouting and howling every night at 10 p.m. in that neighborhood. The collective screaming is said to be good for students as they let off steam! Maybe it is not quite that good for other residents. Don´t be copy cats and introduce it in Manhattan or Miami.

Flygskam (Flight-shaming)

This environmental movement grew strong in the wake of Greta Thunberg´s campaign for a better culture. It wants travelers to stop flying to reduce the CO2 emission. Swedes fly 7 times more than average global citizens but the total CO2 emissions have fallen by 24% since 1990. Unfortunately air traffic has grown meanwhile by more than 60%. The idea of flight-shaming is to make people feel ashamed to fly since it has such a negative impact on the world and our climate. Researchers and prominent people have agreed that flying is wrong and have cut down on flying. They have stopped taking off and have started taking in - the truth.

[The] Swede

Flygskam. Flight-shaming has been part of the official list of Swedish words since 2017. The moral of air travel has been widely discussed in Sweden in recent years. Some claim that emissions from air traffic are so great that it is almost an obligation to choose means of transport that do not pose as much impact on the environment.

Folk music

(See Music) The old folk music tradition lives on and is thriving. In some rural areas its grip on old and young people is still strong. Provinces like Dalarna and Hälsingland have thousands of musicians who play in groups or in larger orchestras.

Dalarna, where old traditions in all shapes are being kept alive, has its "spelmän" (musicians) The violin also plays a vital role. At Midsummer these musicians in their old costumes entertain people from all over the province. Folk music goes from happy-sing-along ditties to melancholic tunes. Many are instrumental. Lyrics often deal with traditional life in the countryside. Cities also have their old songs, like Stockholm and its bard Bellman (18th century).

Folk parks

Folk parks (folkparker), public entertainment parks, have been in existence since 90% of the Swedes lived in the countryside, there were farms all over, cars were rare and maids were made pregnant by farmhands. There are fewer parks today but they will hopefully live on, although in new shapes, adapted to modern and city life.

Generally the folk park area is fenced in to stop youngsters from getting in without paying. There is a small stage and a dance floor. In the stalls coffee, non-alcoholic beverages and hot dogs are sold. The music may vary from Svensktoppsmusic (See Svensktoppen!) to light pop or even rock. Frank Sinatra, believe it or not, went on tour in the 1950s and performed at some of the folk parks.

Food

Typical domestic specialties today are pizza, spaghetti, burgers, Chinese food and sushi. In other words, visitors to Sweden will survive, probably also enjoy and recognize the meals.

Mother's meatballs, grandfather's pigs' tails and Uncle Bo's black pudding are having a hard time. No wonder—what food can compete with the Italian, French or Asian cuisine? Sometimes though,

[The] Swede

Fredagsmys.

you will experience a "gående bord," a kind of buffet.

Swedes eat a lot of fresh food, too. Americans might think Swedes serve their vegetables raw, but chefs and cooks all over the blue-and-yellow country would describe them as "al dente." They make a sound when you try to attack them.

An American exchange student in Sweden once said: "I ate less in the States than here in Europe. Yet, I am losing weight!" Well, the amount is not what matters, the content is. With less fat and peanut butter replaced by more salad and crispbread you lose pounds.

If we are talking desserts, then ice cream dominates the scene. Thick, rich puddings do not belong in the weight watchers' world. Sometimes fruit and cheese replace ice cream.

Fredagsmys (Cozy Friday)

In one commercial on TV they sing about "fredagsmys" while eating crisps. And that is basically it. Gather your family around the television set, switch on a family program and drink soda, eat sweets, popcorn, potato chips or fruit. That's fredagsmys, and as the name implies it has got to be on a Friday evening. It is the start of the weekend with the whole family together.

The adults will have to sacrifice other programs, beer, wine and booze. But after their offspring have gone to bed, the party starts with films, Facebook, Instagram or the mothers and fathers are simply socializing with their loyal smartphones.

Genealogy

This popular pastime has a large following in Sweden. For decades people have gathered information about their forefathers. Thanks to the Mormons and their filming of church records, archives all over the country are able to supply researchers with material. The internet has made it easier to contact other people exploring their roots. Church books subscriptions online are possible for an annual fee, the Swedish Death Index 1860-2017 is available, as are population records of say 1950 or 1980.

Americans especially tend to come here to look into their Swedish background. One tip to all of those who are spelling-challenged is to get all the funny names right before you start looking. That will save you folks from a lot of effort that leads to nothing. Using DNA seems to be a favorite way of exploring your history from the days in Africa up to the present.

Generalizations

They should never be encouraged, but are necessary in many cases, like in this book. Of course 10 million inhabitants are individuals. Of course gender and age play a role. Of course conditions vary from city to countryside. They also differ between the north and the south. That is why domestic readers will reject some of the writer's opinions. Still, how else would these pages be possible? The writer has to trust his readers and their ability to distinguish between fun and seriousness, between facts and opinions and their willingness to consult other sources.

Gingerbread house

In thousands of Swedish homes the making of the gingerbread house, either pre-fabricated in sections or baked and assembled in the kitchen, is a fun tradition for both parents and children around Christmas. On the roof of the house belong a couple Smarties, and the whole construction is glued with melted sugar. After Christmas they are consumed by young members of the family or simply thrown away.

God

" ... so help me God," the president of the United States concluded his speech to the nation. In Sweden, neither the king nor the Prime Minister (statsministern) would use the word god, except when they speak Swedish, which they do all the time: "god" simply means "good." Religion is considered everyone's personal and private sphere and is generally treated as such. Not even the leader of the Christian Democrats would utter this word in a public speech.

After almost 500 years, the Swedish State Church and the State went their separate ways on January 1, 2000. Thousands of Swedes have left the church ever since, to avoid paying church tax, because they have no religious belief or simply because they belong to other churches. Even though the country is secular and church-goers fewer and fewer, Jesus would most likely have liked the equality, the treatment of the less fortunate and society taking care of its inhabitants. Maybe Swedes are more religious in daily life than they think.

Gothenburg (Göteborg)

Sweden's second largest town on the estuary of Göta Älv (river) on the west coast of Sweden changed from a busy port with docks employing more than 10,000 workers into an industrial city with Volvo and SKF (ball bearings) as two important enterprises. In the latest phase it has become a white-collar city. With all its parks and green areas, the city also offers Allén, a one-mile stretch of land with lots of tree species. The moat, surrounding the city, is within a stone's throw from Allén. Fiskekyrkan (Fish Church) is a fish market in the shape of a church, hence the name. Couples are known to get married in it.

The Botanical Garden and its neighbor Slottsskogen, the favorite recreational area for Gothenburgers, with lakes, a children's zoo and picnic spots, attract people all year long.

Take a walk along Avenyn (the Avenue) with the art museum at the top at Götaplatsen and the statue of Poseidon having a shower with his fish. Department stores and shops line the street. Riding the museum tram is possible here. Regular trams operate all around Gothenburg. Try them for a relaxing ride! Remember to find out how tickets work before stepping onto one of them or a bus or a ferry. Otherwise you will hate Göteborg.

Kronhusbodarna contain goldsmiths, glass artists, clockmakers, an old fashioned shop and a museum with Gothenburg in miniature.

A boat trip in the harbor on the sightseeing boats Paddan (the

Toad) is top priority. On seafaring boats you may also visit populated islands in the archipelago off the coast of Gothenburg.

A full day at Liseberg, the largest amusement park in Scandinavia and the most popular Swedish tourist attraction, is a good investment for families with younger children. So is Universeum with its rain forest and tropical fish such as sharks.

Scandinavium hosts rock concerts and also ice hockey games by the Frölunda Indians, the pride of the city. Ullevi is the arena, where the World Championship of Football was held in 1958 and has had many events ever since, including concerts by Bruce Springsteen, the Rolling Stones and Ed Sheeran.

Skansen Kronan and Skansen Lejonet are two forts in the town that were erected in the late 17th century. A boat takes tourists to the isle of Älvsborg's fästning (fortress). Götheborg, a replica of the Swedish East Indiaman Götheborg I that sailed to China in the 18th century, actually set sail for Asia in 2004 and it will embark on another voyage, more than 15 years later.

From historical to modern environments you need to get to the huge indoor shopping mall Femman near the port with a great number of large and small shops. And by the time you read this, the first really tall skyscraper, the Karla Tower (Karlatornet), may be in place (estimated late 2022), something that will change the skyline of the city. By the way, there are not many skyscrapers in Sweden. We never compete with mountains.

Gotland

It is Sweden's largest island, in the Baltic. In the old days it belonged to Denmark and the German Order, and since 1645 has been a Swedish province. With its almost 100 churches, most of them built in medieval days, Gotland has its own special atmosphere. The whole island is a museum of culture, history and recreation.

Bunge, with its museum and church, belongs to one of the highlights. Fårö, the island where Ingmar Bergman among others spent many summers, houses a large number of so-called "raukar." These rock formations often have shapes like upright people and can reach

26 feet in height. Hoburgen in the south attracts visitors with its "raukar," especially the famous "old man Hoburg" and its yellow slopes in May full of spring Adonis.

Kattlundsgården, and its medieval barn, is open in the summer like Lummelundagrottan, a system of caves open to visitors.

Visby, the historic and only town on the island, is surrounded by a wall that's two miles long, some of it almost 40 feet high.

The annual Almedalsveckan in early July attracts politicians and lobbyists by the thousands, their every move covered by national media. The Medieval Week in early August with its 500 events and 40,000 visitors gives the town a chance to find its roots, with its inhabitants and visitors dressed in costumes from 600 years back in time. This week is a paradise for lovers of jousting, markets, street theater, fire shows, walks, lectures etc.

Greta

Greta Thunberg was an introverted, bright child, diagnosed with Asperger's. But now the pigtailed, shy girl is a worldwide star. It all started in August, 2018 in Stockholm when then 15-year-old Greta got tired of people with power not taking the climate issue seriously. She decided to do something herself and started a school strike outside Parliament (Riksdagen) until the September 2018 elections. Greta was interviewed by the World Press, got invited by Arnold Schwarzenegger to the R20 meeting in Austria later in the year, to COP24 (24th Conference of the Parties to the UN Convention on Climate Change in Katowice, Poland) as well as the World Economic Forum in Davos, Switzerland. She has met the pope, presidents and prime ministers in an attempt to convince them about the danger of climate changes. She took a leap year after finishing high school to attend the UN climate summit in New York City and the UN Framework Convention on Climate Change in Santiago, Chile in late 2019. She did it her way and left England on a sail boat bound for America. The young Swedish climate activist's protests have aroused great international attention and garnered followers among Generation Z—the group that might pay a steep price for today's and yesterday's mistakes—in the world. Already in January 2019 over 60,000 students around the world were on strike for a better climate. And, she was among the nominees for the Nobel Peace Prize that year.

Gästrikland

This province of coastline and beauty has based its income on timber and ore. Many of its industrial buildings are turned into museums but modern factories like those in Sandviken and Hofors are still operating. Another stop might be Furuvik, south of Gävle, which is a zoo and amusement park.

Gävle, the oldest town in Norrland (the nine northernmost provinces), is a shipping and trading center. Gamla Gefle (Old Gävle) houses a museum dedicated to Joe Hill. He was a trade unionist, a syndicalist, a poet and a singer, who moved to America, and tried to organize workers, but was sentenced to death on unclear grounds in a murder case, which caused mass demonstrations. The traditional giant (approximately 40 feet tall) straw Gävle Julbock (Christmas goat) is heavily guarded these days to prevent people from setting fire to it. It has only survived 16 Christmases out of 52 (2018). Valbo, near Gävle, has kept its old character with farms along the main road.

Göteborg (See Gothenburg)

Halland

This province (not Holland) has been Swedish since 1658, when Denmark had to give it up after a bit of coercion involving diplomatic guns and the like. Four rivers traverse Halland through fertile agricultural areas.

Fjärås bräcka, south of lovely Kungsbacka, contains a long ridge that cuts off the lake from the plain below. A prehistoric grave field adds to the attraction of this place. Äskhult's by (village), southeast of Kungsbacka, is a piece of 18th century Sweden with the whole village preserved in its old shape.

Halmstad, the biggest town in Halland, offers nice pedestrian zones and places to eat. The sandy beaches of Tylösand not far from the town, and Laholm, the oldest and most picturesque town in Halland, all make this an interesting part of the province.

Varberg, summer town and swimming resort, has a castle dating back to the days when the province was part of the Danish nation. The history museum inside simply has to be seen.

Morups Tånge, near the pretty town of Falkenberg with its sandy beaches, offers unique possibilities to see migrating birds. Ringhals kärnkraftverk (Ringhals Nuclear Power Station) is clearly seen on the coastline. This ensures that you can see the birds at night thanks to their fascinating glow. Swedes think of everything!

HBTQ

Sweden is a tolerant country when it comes to different aspects of life. As for HBTQ-questions, the county has hosted Europride three times. Most important, Sweden has more than 30 pride-related events annually. The government, local politicians and members of Parliament frequently take part in the parades and celebrations. In 2019 the country celebrated its 75th anniversary of the decriminalization of homosexuality. This does not mean that the situation for homosexuals, bisexuals, trans- and queer people is a garden of roses. Prejudice is a hard nut to crack but with the right tools it is possible.

H&M

This is a clothing retail company for men, women, teenagers and children. H&M operates in more than 60 countries with over 4,500 stores. It employs far more than 100,000 people. It is in the Top Five clothing retailers in the world.

Hej

You say "Hej" (pronounced hey) when you meet someone. That goes for everybody, including His Majesty the King and any politician, tycoon or celebrity.

Swedes are very informal and would never say "God dag" or anything like that. Of course "God morgon" or "God kväll/God afton" (good evening) are accepted, but can easily be avoided. They may be used on television or by the staff of a restaurant.

Among young people "Tjenare" is a colloquial way of putting it, even "Tjabba". But refrain from using them. You are not 15 anymore or am I wrong? Also, remember "god" means "good". "Gud" means "God".

Hen

This kind of hen does not lay many eggs. No, this is a new gender-neutral personal pronoun. It can be used instead of the words hon (she) and han (he). Instead of writing "I don't know where he or she is" you could write "I don't know where hen is," indicating that you don't care whether it is a he or a she, or merely because you are lazy. "I have a friend. Do you know hen?"

Hollywood stars (Swedish)

Greta Garbo and Ingrid Bergman probably started the Swedish saga of Hollywood. In the modern world of film, Swedish actresses like Alicia Vikander (2016 Oscar winner), Malin Åkerman, Noomi Rapace, Izabella Scorupco, Rebecca Ferguson, Lena Olin and Tuva Novotny have taken part in the Californian circus. Among actors, the Skarsgård family with daddy Stellan, his sons Alexander, Gustav and Bill must be mentioned, Max von Sydow, Michael Nyqvist (1960-2017), Joel Kinnaman and David Dencik are other names out of many.

Among directors Lasse Hallqvist, Tomas Alfredsson, Daniel Espinosa among others have made themselves a name in Hollywood.

Homes

Swedish families pay a lot of attention to keeping their apartments or houses in good shape. Gardens and yards must be spotless with no withering plants, no weeds and no grass longer than 0.2 mm. The exterior walls of a house should look perfect in beautiful colors, often white or possibly red. In some areas houses will be painted every third or fifth year because of weathering from wind and salt.

In an apartment or house, matching colors are of utmost importance. This goes for curtains, bedspreads, toilet seat covers, mugs and plants. Curtains never cover the whole window. They are designed to show off the interior rather than stop people from looking in.

Lights are often on, even when the various members of a family leave a room not to come back until bedtime. When you go to a party you leave some lights on to make it look cozy when you get back.

Lamps are placed in the window, on the living room table, on dressers, bedside tables, in any possible corner. During the dark part of the year, bushes, trees, balconies and garden sheds may have lights as well. Mind you, these are white lights only. Colored lights are supposed to be vulgar or flashy and foreign, according to many Swedes. Blinking multi-colored Christmas lights are not yet approved of, but in due time they will probably be popular and accepted. It is a changing world.

Electricity prices have risen considerably over the last few years. Still, the average Swede prefers to pay his bill over being excluded from this important addition to life. Of course we haven't worked out that you can reduce the costs. Turning off lights is a new idea, a message which energy companies don't exactly spread either. A home should be cozy, because that is where you spend 15 hours a day 350 days a year, is the general idea.

[The] Swede

Husesyn. Going on a walk about around a home the first time you visit is not uncommon. The inspection has little to do with the original meaning of the word and while it might be considered polite to show an interest in a friend's new home, it may be wise to make sure everyone is on the same page ...

Houses

Why are Swedish barns and houses in the countryside—and sometimes in towns—painted red?

Well, originally this product, Falu Rödfärg, was extracted from the Falu copper mine, which was in operation for 700 years. The paint lasts for years and protects timber from rotting. In recent days it has partially been replaced by other sorts of paint, but the color often remains the same—red.

That private homes are made of wood can easily be explained. The supply of timber is extremely good. Larger buildings are made of other material like brick or stone for security reasons. Fires have destroyed so many towns in this country. In the 19th century they devastated town centers in places like Karlstad and Sundsvall.

For security reasons, wood buildings were historically not allowed to be built more than two stories high. Still, Gothenburg has got something called "landshövdingehus" (governors' houses), buildings with one floor of stone and two of wood. This was a clever way of legally cheating the authorities! Three for the price of two. Today, wood is used more and more, for multi-family homes, gymnasiums, hotels and public buildings.

Housewives

This phenomenon hardly exists anymore. Swedish women work outside their homes more than in most European countries. The figure is about 80%.

Although Swedish men are said to be active in their homes, doing their share of the chores, a heavy responsibility still lies on the wives.

Maybe the Japanese guest at a Swedish family, who took a large number of digital photos of the host in his apron, should have directed his camera toward the hostess instead. She is the one who struggles at work and then at home, a combination which takes its toll.

Hugging

Three or four decades ago, the Swedish population was inhibited as far as touching is concerned. You shook hands with somebody—and that was it.

Today, after having received more than one million immigrants, habits have changed. Hugging takes place everywhere, anytime and anyhow. Even older generations have adopted this way of greeting or parting. The whole population seems to have melted and has become good Europeans continental style. Do not be surprised if you are a man in your 50s and the daughter of your host family hugs you on arrival and on departure. It is natural.

Humor

If you were by chance to ask a Danish citizen to describe a typical Swede, the answer might be as follows: a boring, stiff and law-abiding teetotaller with no sense of humor. Were you, however, to ask a Swede the same question, the reply would differ greatly insofar as he would say: a boring, stiff and law-abiding average drinker. A sense of humor? Well??

Swedish humor can best be described by quoting a British TV producer who affirmed: "When we want to test a new comedy show abroad we turn to Israel and Sweden. They have a kind of humor similar to ours." Any British comedy or series will be successful in the land of the blue and yellow flag. As for American equivalents, the chances are somewhat lower. US action comedies on the other hand seem to have a large following.

Gothenburg has a reputation for its humorous inhabitants. Short, snappy jokes are typical in this port. There is an angry woman leaning out of the window, shouting "Two on a bike!" indicating this is not allowed according to the law. One of the boys turns around and replies: "And you sure know how to count, ma'am!" This is funny in Gothenburg, probably nowhere else.

One delicate problem that has arisen affects writers of comedy. Anything is allowed these days. You can make jokes about the king, the clergyman and the average citizen. The forbidden fruit has already been eaten. This makes life harder for comedy writers and comedians.

Husesyn (House inspection)

Since the Middle Ages this is an inspection of leased property that has crept into regular people's lives in a peculiar way; the first time you visit someone's home you would expect to "go husesyn" (literally house inspection) to check out all of the rooms, including bath rooms, any special equipment, available storage areas etc. It is not uncommon for the host to offer new guests a walk around an apartment or a house. It is, however, for the wife of the writer of this book, who dislikes showing guests toothbrushes, closets and dirty clothes in the washing machine. She is a sane representative of Sweden. But to be fair, she may give in to her husband when he wants to show the guests his computer with the genealogy program or the garden. On the other hand, the garden is not in the house.

Hälsingland

This province gets its income from agriculture and forests. Its breathtaking views along lakes and on hills must be seen. Bollnäs has a magnificent view of the river (Ljusnan) and Kämpens, the open-air museum. Hudiksvall attracts tourists with its old Fiskarstaden (Fishermen's town) and Söderhamn has its beautiful part Öster with all the wood houses.

The annual folk music festival draws crowds to Delsbo. Hornslandet, on the Baltic, is a recreational area. Järvsö, a small place, offers Bonarv and Karlsgården and buildings dating back to the 17th century. Last but not least, Ljusdal has an open-air museum and a folk park.

Härjedalen

This is a sparsely populated province that once belonged to Norway (until 1645). It has seen Stone Age trappers on the treeless mountains, the Sami people with their reindeer and pilgrims on their way to Trondheim, Norway. The high snow-covered mountains in the west are typical features of beautiful Härjedalen.

Bruksvallarna has a great number of prehistoric graves and "fäbodar," simple summerhouses for farm girls milking and producing dairy products. In Funäsdalen you will find the oldest open-air museum in the province with a remarkable collection of old houses. Lillhärdal is another example of old, well kept houses and sheds. Finally Sveg, the most important place in the province, makes a good starting point for outings. Its open-air museum offers coffee and ice cream but most of all old buildings. Outdoor activities, including fishing, hiking, climbing and skiing, make Härjedalen a true paradise for active tourists and hell for the lazy ones.

Ice cream

This summer pleasure has turned into a 12-months-a-year craze. Swedes are big ice cream consumers, regardless of season or place. Even on a cold winter's day you see ice cream being eaten in shopping malls.

In July, residents eat various flavors of ice cream in their cars, sidewalk cafés and amusement parks, on boats, in parks and tourist attractions. You will not see them eating ice cream in their homes, but you can bet they eat it there, too. The word "glass" (ice cream) will be heard a lot from the mouths of tiny, small and bigger children.

Ikea

This large, worldwide chain of "do-it-partly-yourself" stores, founded by Ingvar Kamprad (1926-2018), has contributed to the standardization of Swedish homes. The "Billy bookshelf" can be found in hundreds of thousands of sitting rooms and every Swede is an expert on assembling any kind of furniture purchased at Ikea. Luckily enough for the Swedish economy, this know-how is spreading throughout the world. Have you personally got it? Can you assemble the bookshelf or any other piece of furniture without swearing once? Then you are in.

Immigration

Sweden has a long history of immigration. Germans arrived in the medieval days. Finns came to cultivate patches of land in the large forests 400 years ago. Walloons from Flanders (contemporary Belgium) and neighboring areas came to assist in establishing ironworks. A small population of Jews has existed in the country for the last two centuries, since the national ban was lifted.

In modern times, the Italian labor immigrants joined the Finnish newcomers in the 1950s. Yugoslavs arrived in the 60s, and after the coup in Santiago thousands of Chilean families came to settle down in Sweden.

After the fall of the Shah in Persia, Iranians started coming. Turks, often with Kurdish background, make up a large ethnic community here. Wars, civil wars and political reasons have given Sweden new citizens from Iraq, Syria, Afghanistan, Iran, Ethiopia, Eritrea and Somalia. There are more Iraqis living in the town of Södertälje than in the whole of the USA.

Last but not least, other Scandinavians, in particular Norwegians, have been coming for as long as anyone can remember. One must not forget the estimated 21,000 Americans and 28,000 Britons who have settled in Sweden.

To young Swedes and young new Swedes (immigrants or children of immigrants), this melting pot has always existed and represents normal life. However, as far as Sweden is concerned, it is a fairly new phenomenon, only a few decades in fact. In suburbs, riots have occurred and clashes between groups have taken place.

In the mid-60s, a group of students from Värmland (a province) was on the way to Germany on a school trip. As the bus drove along Avenyn, the main street of Göteborg, a student rushed to the window, camera in hand, shouting: "Look! A Negro!! A Negro!" (This word was used then.) No one in the coach had ever seen one.

Today the same students, now respected citizens, will see khimars and hijabs on women's heads and also burqas, niqabs and chadors covering their bodies in suburbs and city centres all over the country. And they will definitely not shout: "Look! An Arab!! An Arab!"

Internet

The internet and social media have changed the world—and people. Instead of watching the world around you, inhabitants of all ages stare at their tiny screen, fully isolated from the surrounding environment.

If you want to pay your parking fee, you use your phone. When you want to exchange money with friends you use Swish as well as in a shop. In many Swedish department stores, a cashless society has been building up for the last years. That is why a lot of Swedes do not recognize their own currency. On the few occasions when it is still used, the poor inhabitants have a problem identifying the various coins. They will have to be twisted and studied in their hands before paying. One explanation is that the internet in Sweden is used by 94% of the population (2018). So why use coins?

Inventions and discoveries

What has a small country of about 10 million inhabitants contributed to the world? Well, the plumber wrench, the (computer) mouse, Ericsson mobile phones, Hasselblad cameras (the first ones in space), the carpenter's rule and the ball bearing, to mention a few in no particular order, originate from Sweden. Other inventions include the zipper, the Tetra Pak, the implantable pacemaker, the three-point seatbelt, medical ultrasound, a tracking ships device and the HIV tracker.

Linné's arranging of plants in systematic families, Celsius centigrade thermometer, Dahlén's lighthouse and the Gripen military plane (JAS) are other examples of successful achievements. The gifted Alfred Nobel exchanged oil and dynamite for prizes. The Greyhound Company, the Coca Cola bottle, Ikea, Saab, Volvo, the propeller and the Monitor have Swedish parents as do in more recent years Minecraft, Skype and Spotify.

iPads (and other electronic devices) at school

In many schools throughout the country, students of all ages are given access to iPads, laptops or similar devices free of charge. Young children, aged 9 - 10, may have iPads, often replacing schoolbooks, and are free to use them at home and at school for as long as they go to that particular school. Afterward they may pay a sum of money to keep it, and, if not, simply hand it in. Older students often get a Mac or some other brand in a system similar to that of the younger pupils above.

The consequences for regular schoolbooks are huge. You cannot have computers AND books. This has alarmed teachers who want to stick to books and other material made of solid wood, instead of numbers 0 and 1. The debate and its pros and cons will rage on forever. It is also a question of discipline. How can you control a bunch of kids with laptops and cellphones in a classroom?

Jordgubbar (Strawberries)

Swedish summers include herring, which is not popular among everyone, but also strawberries, which is popular among everyone.

As for strawberries there is one must. They have to be Swedish. In average Swedes consume 40 million liters, about 4 – 5 liters per person (including new-born babies and people older than 100 years. They (not the babies or oldies) are sold along roads and streets on temporary tables or in supermarkets until late July or early August. The exact meaning of the word is "jord" (earth or dirt) and "gubbar" (old men). Who said that Swedish is a normal language?

Jämtland

It has been part of Sweden since 1645 after having belonged to Norway (in its turn ruled by Denmark!). Storsjön, the big lake, is to this province what Lake Siljan is to Dalarna, i.e. the center of the province. To the west you have mountains with winter sports in places like the well-known Åre resort. Around Storsjön you will find the cultural and administrative heart of Jämtland. The railway to Trondheim in Norway has promoted tourism and today the province relies on visitors for much of its income.

Frösön, an island in Lake Storsjön, was during earlier centuries the place where justice was done, where the "governor" lived and where markets took place. A zoo and an observation tower belong to the popular sights on the island. Hoverberget (Hover Mountain) gives the tourist a splendid view of parts of Jämtland, unless you are in one of its caves, of course.

Ragundadalen (Ragunda Valley) with Döda fallet (the Dead Waterfall) has an interesting history. About 200 years ago Lake Ragunda was emptied completely by humans, a great mistake, and that is how the Dead Fall came about. Ånnsjön (Lake Ånn) has an entry in the international list of protected areas. Rock carvings, areas for the protection of birds and Stone Age dwellings can be studied there.

In Östersund, the only town in Jämtland, the visitor ought to visit Jämtli, the local museum with the presumed oldest tapestry in Europe (9th–10th centuries). The pretty town stretches out on the slopes of the lake. Rumor has it that the equivalent of Nessie, the Loch Ness monster, hides in the dark waters of Lake Storsjön. Adults never grow up.

Kalles kaviar

It is a Swedish brand of fish roe spread that, despite its name, is not comparable to regular caviar. Its main ingredients are tomato sauce, fish roe and sugar; it comes in a tube and is spread like toothpaste (refrain from brushing your teeth with this, however). Kalles kaviar has been a commercial success in Sweden ever since its market launch in 1954, but attempts to win customers in other cultures have been hard. Some PR-consultant had the bright idea of offering this fish roe to passers-by in New York City, showing their faces of disgust in the TV-commercial. It was no great success. The tube has maintained the same design from the beginning, depicting the son of the then CEO of the manufacturing company. The tube design is easily recognizable and has become a symbol of 1950's nostalgia in Sweden. Today it is owned by a Norwegian company along with

Abba´s herring (not ABBA the pop group), Ballerina biscuits, Önos jam and Bob juice, those gems of Swedish goodies.

Kilometers and miles

"How far is Alingsås from here?" a British subject asked.

"About nine miles, Sir!"

"All right, then I'll walk."

"You can't do that, Sir!"

"Why not?"

"It's too far. It would take you 18 hours."

What can we learn from this conversation? Well, Swedes tend to use the word "mile" or a "Swedish mile," which corresponds to 10,000 meters or ten kilometers. So when they say "nine miles" they mean 90 km and not 14.4 km. If you need to convert kilometers into miles to know how long the next leg of your tour will be, follow the advice below, although it does not give the exact distance.

Distance: 90 kilometers: Reduce 90 by a third (90 to 30), then double it and you will get the approximate mileage = 60 miles.

- Distance: 60 kilometers: 60 to 20 = approximately 40 miles
- Distance: 110 kilometers: 110 to 37 = approximately 70 miles

Exercises while traveling — convert into miles:

1. Sweden from the North to the South: 1,574 km
2. The widest part of Sweden: 499 km
3. Malmö to Göteborg (Gothenburg) 278 km
4. Göteborg to Stockholm 482 km
5. Stockholm to Sundsvall 398 km
6. Sundsvall to Kiruna 866 km

Kilos and pounds

The pound (0.45 kg) and ounce (28.35 grams) are less commonly understood in Sweden. One ton in Sweden is 1,000 kg and not 2,000 pounds (907 kg as in America) or 1016 kg (as in Britain). The writer of this text does not understand math at all, so you had better look it up online.

When in Sweden, stick to kilos while explaining your weight. If you are very fussy about the exact kilos, use a calculator. If you do not pay that much attention to exactness, simply take half the weight of your pounds and you will get a slightly higher weight than in real life.

Example: If you weigh 200 pounds, say: 100 kg (the exact sum is actually 90 kg). If you weigh 160 pounds, say: 80 kg (the exact weight is 72 kg).

Kings and Queens

Swedish history has more than its share of kings (and queens) since the country was a monarchy for over one thousand years. Don't try to make sense of the numbers, however, the amount of King Karls and Eriks are somewhat hard to follow prior to the 16th century.

Birger Jarl

He lived from about 1210 to 1266 and played an important role in the foundation of Sweden as a nation. Birger also established Swedish rule in Finland, which would not end until 1809 when Russia defeated Sweden and ruled the Finns until 1917. Birger Jarl is by many regarded as the founder of Stockholm

Margareta I

Margareta Valdemarsdotter was born in 1353 and died in the plague 1412. She was queen of Denmark and Norway for 25 years and Sweden for 23 years. Iceland, the Faroe Islands and Greenland were part of the Danish rule. Additionally she ruled over Finland, then part of Sweden. In other words, she reigned over the Nordic countries.

Gustav Vasa (See Vasa, Gustav)

Gustavus II Adolphus

He lived from 1594 to 1632. Gustavus is often called the founder of Sweden as a great European power, thanks to his great success in the Thirty Years' War. On a personal level it was not, as he was killed at the Battle of Lützen in today's Germany. He introduced parish registration as a means of controlling taxes and making sure that conscription worked.

(See more under Vasa, Gustav.)

Queen Kristina

She was the last member of the Vasa Dynasty. Kristina (1626-1689) is said to have been witty and intelligent. She sponsored the arts in an attempt to make Stockholm "the Athens of the North" and had a lot of influence when it comes to European culture. Financially she more or less ruined her country. In 1654 she abdicated, converted to Roman Catholicism and left for Rome where she soon fell out with the Pope, who described her as "a Christian without faith, and a woman without shame". Despite this criticism she stayed there all her life.

Karl XII

Born in 1682 he came to power in 1697. He spent a lot of his time in wars. Initially he was very successful and won victories like the Battle of Narva (Estonia today) against the Russian czar Peter the Great. Karl XII marched on Moscow, like Napoleon and Hitler later on, with the same result. He was defeated and spent the following years in the Ottoman Empire before riding back to Sweden through Europe. Once home, Karl XII attacked Norway but was shot at the siege of Fredriksten (at Halden) in 1718. Was he shot by his own soldiers or by a Norwegian bullet? The answer remains a secret.

Gustav III

If Karl XII was a warrior, Gustav III was a defender of the arts. He founded the Swedish Academy. Gustav seized power from the government in a coup d'état but welcomed a new one aimed to represent all citizens. He legalized Catholic and Jewish presence in the country. Gustav was the first head of state to recognize the United States. In 1792 he was shot at a masquerade ball in Stockholm and died from the wounds a couple of days later.

Bernadotte

The royal house of Sweden, the Bernadottes, has reigned since 1818. Sweden lost Finland in 1809 but forced Norway into a union in 1814 that lasted until 1905. Jean Bernadotte, former high-ranked officer in the Napoleon army, now Swedish and Norwegian king under the name of Karl XIV Johan, was the first of many kings of this family.

Charles XVI Gustav (born in 1946) succeeded his parental grandfather on the throne in 1973 and was still king in 2019. His daughter, Crown princess Victoria born in 1977, will succeed him in due time. She is a popular princess who spends time doing charity and is celebrated each year on her birthday with thousands of spectators at the summer palace Solliden on the isle of Öland. The show is televised. She has a husband and two children. So, for more than 200 years, the Bernadottes have reigned over the country in the North. That is, they have a formal role these days. Democracy reigns.

Knäckebröd

Crisp, hard rye bread has been eaten by the Swedish population for hundreds of years. It comes in many shapes. The big, round thin ones with a large hole in the middle used to hang from the ceiling in many peasants' homes in earlier centuries. Today you purchase it in supermarkets in every shape possible. Look for the word "knäckebröd" on the shelves. It tastes good and has a healthy effect on your stomach.

Korvkiosk

Fast food and McDonald's exist in Sweden, but if you'd rather have a snack the Swedish way, try a "korvkiosk" (hot dog stand or cart) instead. Of course you will find the inevitable burgers there too, but stick to the hot dog as they are better, right?

"En hel special" or "en halv special" might be a suitable choice. You'll get either two sausages ("hel") or just one (halv) in a bun with "mos" (mashed potatoes) on top to go with it. As a "topping" you may want pickles, mustard or ketchup. Study the colored illustrations of different extras and point at something of your liking.

Lagom

The Swedish word "lagom" has in many cases been used as a word to describe the Swedish mentality. Its meaning can be said to be "just about right" or "no more no less." Everything in Sweden should be lagom. There is even a brand of margarine called Lätt & Lagom (light and just about right). You should drink alcoholic beverages in lagom doses. Your kids should be raised with a lagom mixture of kindness and strictness.

The length of this explanation is probably lagom by now. The title of the book could have been Lagom, a lagom introduction to Swedes and Sweden.

Language, the Swedish

Swedish has its roots in the Indo-European language group, like English, German, French, Spanish, Italian and Dutch. As an English-speaking person you should refrain from using words like "idiot," "imbecile," "shit" or "fuck" when there are Swedes around. They will understand and immediately take for granted that you are talking about them, which you probably are.

Norwegian sounds more like Swedish and is understood by most Swedes. There are difficult dialects though, just like in Sweden.

Danish and Swedish are closely connected languages. Swedes today though, seem to prefer to speak English while in Denmark. The language of this neighboring country is said to be unclear, with a guttural tone to it, which of course is not true. In written form it does not constitute that much of a problem for a Swede.

Finnish has no resemblance to practically any Western European language. You may compare Gaelic to English to understand the difference. About 290,000 Finns in Finland, so-called Swedish Finns, have Swedish as their mother tongue. But the number is decreasing. Finnish-speaking Finns prefer English over Swedish as their second language in schools.

Lappland (Lapland)

This last wilderness of Europe with tall mountains, the Sami people, sparsely populated valleys and open plains, is the northernmost province of Sweden. The large findings of iron ore in Gällivare and Kiruna made Lapland attractive to settlers. The railway, linking the mines with Norway, made them profitable.

Kebnekaise, Sweden's tallest mountain, can be reached by experienced climbers. Sarek, a national park, boasts a breathtaking landscape and almost 90 peaks higher than 5,900 feet. Stora Sjöfallet, another national park, is the third largest in Sweden. Abisko, a fourth national park, close to the Norwegian border, offers dry climate with rare vegetation. Kungsleden, the 30-mile-long trail, takes you on a trek all the way to Ammarnäs (a genuine mountain village).

Correct clothing, good shoes, plenty of food, water and mosquito spray and off you go! Hemavan offers trails, skiing facilities and the observation tower Kung Karl (King Charles). In Jokkmokk, the market, and Ájtte, the Mountain and Sami Museum, introduce tourists to the world of traditional Samiland (Lapland).

Jukkasjärvi, near Kiruna, invites you to the sensational Ice Hotel with its ice sculptures, ice bar and ice beds. There is also an open-air museum nearby in the village. Kiruna, said to be the world's largest town, stretches from Norway to Finland but has less than 23,000 inhabitants, of which about 18,000 live in the town of Kiruna. The borough covers more than 7,700 square miles. The whole town is being moved two miles because the iron mine is making the town an unsafe place to live in. Yes, you got it right. They are moving Kiruna, building a new town center and new homes, in addition to the houses and buildings they've already moved on trucks. The winding paths down into the iron ore mine won't move, however.

Letters to the editor

These letters vary from poetry to messages from 3-year-olds (although they in reality are adults). In most papers, "ordinary people" complain about just anything. Smelly dogs, gravel on the pavement, too much water in the river, bad politicians, wrong government, not enough water in the river, lousy TV shows and expensive milk. In other words, Swedes are just like other human beings worldwide.

Lindgren, Astrid

She was a popular writer, born in 1907 and deceased in 2002. Astrid Lindgren, creator of Pippi Longstocking, achieved stardom at an early stage of her career. Her books about Emil, the mischievous but charming little boy in rural Småland, are part of the Swedish literary heritage. We are all raised on her books. The Russians took Karlsson on the Roof to heart, and Mio My Mio and Brothers Lionheart are other bestselling books by her.

Astrid Lindgren fought for animal rights all her life. She got involved in politics by protesting about the over 100% tax that she paid. Her protest led to changes in taxation in Sweden. In the town of Vimmerby, Småland, Astrid Lindgren´s World offers 50 performances every day in the lovely park with the living settings based on her books. Astrid has been translated into a great many major languages, so make sure you get a copy of one of her books to take back to youngsters in your family or neighborhood.

Lingonberries

This red berry grows in abundance in forests. Bitter as it is, it makes an excellent berry to be included in dishes like meatballs. They say it works as well as cranberries as a condiment to your Thanksgiving turkey in the U.S. Swedes do not generally use it for dessert. It can be purchased in any supermarket. Look for lingon, or even better, for lingonsylt (jam).

Licorice, salty

How about an ice cream with licorice coating? Or black licorice flavored ice cream? It is liked by children and adults, and hated by children and adults who don't know how to enjoy life.

Literature

This lighthearted book is not the right forum for presenting Swedish Literature, like Olof von Dalin, Johan Henrik Kellgren, Anna Maria Lenngren in the 18th century, or Esaias Tegnér, Gustaf Geijer, Carl Jonas Love Almqvist, August Strindberg and Gustaf Fröding in the 19th century. Verner von Heidenstam, Hjalmar Söderberg, Elin Wägner, Hjalmar Bergman, Dan Andersson, Pär Lagerkvist and Harry Martinsson are other Swedish authors.

Vilhelm Moberg, Fritiof Nilsson "Piraten," Stig Dagerman, Tomas Tranströmer, Astrid Lindgren, Sven Delblanc, Lars Norén and dozens of others in the 20th century will have to be found elsewhere. So will all the internationally known writers of detective stories, action and Nordic Noir, such as Stieg Larsson (The Millennium series), David Lagercrantz (who writes new Millennium books after Stieg Larsson's death), Henning Mankell (inspector Wallander), Camilla Läckberg, Leif G.W. Persson and Håkan Nesser are successful too.

Liters

To an American, one gallon is 3.79 liters, to a Brit 4.52 litres. See the problem? To a Swede a liter is a liter at the gas station. Period.

To understand the Swedish price of gasoline an American tourist will have to multiply by a high digit to compare prices with U.S. gas stations. No matter how it's counted, the price in Sweden far exceeds that of the equivalent in the States anyway. (Check prices online.) British or Irish tourists who inquire about petrol, may expect a slightly higher price. Prices at Swedish petrol stations are just a bit more expensive than in the UK.

As for pints, no one cares about the exact figure. It is a question of minutes before the beer has disappeared down your throat anyway. Should you however wish to get involved in a discussion with a Swedish pub guest, tell him or her that a pint in America is slightly less than 5 decilitres and closer to 6 decilitres in the UK. If you want to be punched on the nose, say that Swedish beer tastes like water. If you don´t, say that you love it and you will make friends.

Lobster premiere

The first Monday after September 20 is Lobster Day. As of 7 a.m. you are allowed to start fishing. The craze on the West Coast is tremendous. The lobster pot may be used by professionals and amateurs. It is heavily regulated when it comes to size and number. In 2018 the first catch rendered the fisherman 83,000 kronor (US $8,800) per kilo at the traditional auction in Gothenburg.

Loppis (Flea market)

These garage sales, car boot sales and yard sales take place all over Sweden, especially in the summer. Some are temporary and pop up when people clean their houses and want to get rid of their garbage and decide to let other poor sods buy them. Others are permanent. The quality can vary from antiques to somebody's old handkerchief or used razor blades. Some are organized markets where you can have your stall and sell your products for the price you decide is correct. It is merely a question of shifting useless goods from one person to another, but the funny thing is that it makes people happy, so why not?

Lucia

This originally Italian saint probably hasn't a lot to do with the celebration of Lucia the Swedish way. Every year in Sweden around mid December, Lucias are crowned in schools, in towns, in big cities and on the national stage.

It is one of the darkest periods of the year. That is why in most cases a blond Lucia, the symbol of light, will be selected to make us think of brighter days. The tradition is slowly fading out since interest has decreased.

A number of girls, seven or eight, are selected. Every local paper then asks readers to choose their favorite. The lucky girl will be crowned in the local main square or elsewhere in her white clothes and illuminated crown. She and her "bridesmaids," and often a gin-

[The] Swede

Lucia.

gerbread man or star boy (a boy with a funny looking high hat and a stick with a star on it), will then spend two weeks visiting factories, offices, official buildings and homes for the elderly in order to raise money for charity. They come in a procession, singing "Santa Lucia," each member with a candle (electric or real) in their hand, singing a couple hymns or carols, reading a few rhymed verses, and singing "Santa Lucia" again as they leave.

Every year Nobel Prize winners get this treatment in their hotel rooms, with coffee and ginger bread. There is one example of a laureate who was frightened by the appearance of these angels dressed in white. It led to a discussion where this tradition was put under heavy fire.

Teenagers use the occasion as an excuse to arrange parties called "lusse-discos." Quite a few dress up in some kind of Father Christmas clothing or part thereof. Girls often have glittering Christmas decorations in their hair. Rumor has it that they get drunk during this long night.

Läxrut

To pay someone or a business to help you with your homework is a fairly new phenomenon. This service was even subsidized by the government, which started a debate about it being right or wrong. It is now abolished. Should those who can afford it pay professionals for this service? Should others not have the same opportunity? Shouldn't schools themselves assist students—without outsiders making money on students and their families?

Lördagsgodis (Saturday candy)

(Also see Candy.) In many Swedish families, Saturday is Family Day. You take your children to the nearest candy store where they fill their little paper bags with all kinds of sweet treats. In most cases they will have to wait until after dinner before they can open them. For adults this is a good opportunity to include a bag of their own or steal the best ones from the defenseless children.

Making fun

Making fun of celebrities is an international phenomenon. In Sweden nothing is holy. Politicians have been portrayed as "the boy" (because of his boyish looks), midgets, having speech impediments (one politician having to repeat the way he speaks, listening to an impersonator in a TV-show telling the member of Parliament how to say it).

The King's "Let's turn over a new leaf" when his days as a young nightclub visitor were in focus became viral. On the King's 50th birthday, a performance by Swedish comedian Robert Gustafsson, getting his manuscript in the wrong order as part of the act, sneezing and clearing his throat, and explaining the difference between a president and a king (who is the son of his father), made the two princesses roar with laughter.

When a former prime minister's face was described as a shoe in a comedy show on TV, he started wearing a badge on his lapel in the shape of a shoe. Another prime minister appeared in a sketch on television, sitting at a meeting, when a man comes in and wants to know who has forgotten to put his dirty cup in the dishwasher. The prime minister, who claims the dishwasher was full, is asked to empty it. In this way he and the "shoe" turned mock into victory. Politicians are human and sometimes/often have a sense of humor.

Medelpad

Agriculture, iron and timber are symbols of this pretty province. Sundsvall, 400 years old, was the town of a large number of sawmills in the 20th century and once cleverly described in the phrase:"Saw by saw I saw wherever I saw" by a visitor. After a devastating fire in 1888 the "stone town" replaced the town of wood buildings. Kulturmagasinet, a former warehouse, today houses a museum, library and archives. Visitors can reach Alnön, an island near Sundsvall, via an impressive bridge. For those interested in prehistoric days and old churches, this is the place to be. Gudmundstjärn, a farm consisting of more than 20 buildings from the

18th century, is open in the summer. Njurunda, a pretty place, offers a church, a rune stone, a prehistoric grave and in the vicinity lakes, fishing villages and moors with orchids.

Mentality

It is impossible to describe average Swedes, but the writer of this book will have a go anyway. At first sight Swedes may look reserved and uninterested. Simply give them time and they will turn into good friends. Exchange students are often of this opinion. Usually they turn into loyal, friendly and trustworthy beings. When they get going they are talkative and caring. If they promise a card for Christmas, it will arrive.

At parties or other gatherings, do not wait for something to happen, because it might not. Approach guests and forget the fact that you are an outsider. Go for it! Do not blabber away too long, though. Give them a chance to fill in a few words between your wise small talk.

Swedes tended to be formal and aware of their social status until say the 70s. Back then elegant ladies were supposed to wear fur coats, men would converse and charm women, children were told exactly what to do and say or be quiet. The man sitting to the right of the party hostess had to make a speech. You phoned the hostess within seven days and thanked her for a beautiful evening.

Today the extreme opposite seems to reign. Be natural. Do not show off by driving an expensive car or wearing fancy clothes. Adopt an average attitude toward life and everything in it. "The Swedes are very easy-going," a French teacher visiting a Swedish upper secondary school exclaimed. "Everything is so informal."

A certain melancholy exists in Sweden just the way it does in the rest of the world. Why shouldn't it? Lagom Swedes can´t always be laughing gnomes, especially not during our long dark winters.

#MeToo

#MeToo hit Sweden like a sledgehammer. Women all over the country organized meetings and discussions. Soon the biggest Swedish women's movement since the early 1900s involved women from show business, the arts, clergy, military, law, media, sports and politics. By the end of this tidal wave, even the illustrious Swedish Academy was shaking in its foundations after allegations about sexual harassment by the spouse of one of the Academy members. This led to the announcement that there would be no Nobel Prize for Literature in 2018 due to the scandal. Adding to that, members left the Academy. New ones now sit on their numbered chairs (1-18).

Midnight sun

North of the Arctic Circle conditions are exceptional. From daylight 24 hours a day in June to 22 hours of night in December is reality for many Swedes, depending on latitude. The further north the more extreme the difference in daylight is. Even in the south, like in Gothenburg, a January day starts at 8:55 a.m. and ends at 13:35 p.m.; in the summer, June 21 starts at 4:11 a.m. and finishes at 10:15 in the evening (the difference being that Gothenburg has 6 hours 40 minutes of daylight on January 1 and 18 hours 4 minutes on June 21).

Midsummer

The longest day of the year is celebrated all over the country. There is a "maypole" on a field in every place, decorated with flowers and twigs from birches or other trees. An accordion player, a couple of violin players and a "leader" will make sure that every member of the family dances around the pole. People will be "hopping like little frogs," and "this is how the boys act and this is how the girls act" will be sung among a number of other special songs. Traditional food, like herring, is consumed. In the evening young people, some well over 20, start celebrating. Keep your eyes closed or do not tell your countrymen what you have witnessed. It is not always a pretty sight.

Migration 2015

In the autumn of 2015, the tide of migrants across Europe came as a big surprise. It led to consequences for Sweden, a country of 10 million inhabitants (2018): 39,196 refugees entered the country in October alone. It was the highest number in one month. For a country that accepted a total of 163,000 migrants that fall and 181,890 in the entire year, the situation created problems.

Midsummer is really all about perspective.

People affected by war and terrorism prior to that were already a heavy burden, although the Swedish people were sympathetic to them. Tens of thousands had to leave in the aftermath of this disaster. It is another story. The situation led to even a bigger rise in the fairly new political party, the earlier mentioned Sverigedemokraterna, "the Sweden Democrats."

They demanded a strict policy on migration.

Military defense

Being a neutral nation in no alliance, Sweden saw the birth of a strong defense decades ago. With the Cold War and the Iron Curtain close to her border, Sweden simply had to invest tax money in the army, the air force and the navy. In the early 60s the Swedish air force was the fourth strongest in the world. Conscription made it possible to draft young men year after year.

The collapse of the Soviet-Union drastically changed the situation. The need for heavy investments in arms seemed less important. Cuts in expenses led to a minor organization with fewer soldiers. The growth of NATO made it next to impossible to justify a strong, expensive defense. Sweden today is surrounded by NATO (Norway, the Baltic countries, Poland, Germany and Denmark). The changing situation in Russia has led to a discussion about the Swedish defense. Invest more money in it or join NATO? The Isle of Gotland, as a consequence of the new geopolitical situation, recently introduced troops and equipment again after many years without any defense at all.

Milk

Swedish families with children spend more money on milk in a week than a Canadian or a UK community does in a year. With three boys in their teens, one mother explained they buy 22 liters weekly (about 6 gallons). Do not be surprised to see fully grown men or women drinking a glass of milk with their lunch as well. It is part of the Swedish way of thinking in "health terms."

A famous Swedish comedian and novel writer, Jonas Gardell, wrote a show about this country, titled "In the Land of Medium-Milk." When it comes to milk, the selection is large. "Red" milk (carton with a red label) contains more fat than "green" milk or "organic" milk. The hardest part occurs when you have to rip off one corner of the carton to open it. It takes a lot of training and invariably cursing as well. That is probably why plastic circular "tops" have been introduced.

Moberg, Vilhelm

This author, who lived from 1898 to 1973, made soldiers in the 19th century real people to most Swedes through "Raskens," who was a soldier.

In his epic work "The Emigrants," "The Immigrants," "The Settlers" and "The Last Letter to Sweden," he taught the Swedes what leaving your country means. Karl-Oskar and Kristina are simply good portraits of the over one million Swedes that left due to famine and failure of the crop and went to America. These books created by Moberg were voted "Books of the Millennium" in Sweden. They are translated into English.

Björn Ulvaeus and Benny Andersson, former ABBA members, wrote a successful musical "Kristina från Duvemåla" based on books by Vilhelm Moberg. It was performed in Sweden and abroad. Emigrants will understand this universal story.

Mobile preschools

If you happen to see a bus driving little kids, it might be one of our more than 40 preschools on wheels. They contain children about 4-5 years of age, spending their days in this moving school. Usually they travel for 30-40 minutes to reach the goal of that particular day's outing.

On one day the children might spend up to six hours out of their ordinary preschool. The destination could be a park, a lake or a forest, where the little ones explore the world by studying fish, mushrooms, insects or whatever is available. Each bus has an interior that contains a play area, children's seats, tables, a kitchenette and facilities to heat their lunches. They are supervised by three or four teachers. And yes, rumor has it there is one in Colorado, USA, also.

By the way, the maximum fee a family pays for child care is 1,425 kronor, approximately $145 a month (October 2018) for the first child. You pay less for the next child and even less for the third toddler. You are also entitled to a combined total of 480 days of parental leave per child.

Modern Myths

- All Swedes are blue-eyed and blond. (No way, not even a majority.)
- Winters in Sweden are harsh and long. (It differs widely from north to south, from inland to coast.)
- Everyone is a socialist. (The Left, former communist, party usually gets 5-8% of the votes in elections.)
- The midnight sun shines all over the place. (Only in the far north where practically no one lives.)
- Polar bears roam the streets. (There is not one single wild specimen in the country.)
- It is impossible for a foreigner to learn to speak Swedish. (Sjutusensjuhundra sjuksköterskor would not agree.)
- Swedes do not drink tea. (In fact more than half the population consumes tea occasionally.)
- Swedes are suicidal. (The number of people who kill themselves has sunk to a much lower level than a few decades ago. In 2012 Sweden landed in the 60th spot globally and approximately 1,200–1,500 people commit suicide annually. In fact, the number was 1,544 in 2017, out of which 355 cases were not established.

- The Swedish sin is a fact. (Well, no more than in Germany, UK, the USA, Brazil or Australia.)

- Swedes are atheistic. (On the Isle of Gotland (57,000 inhabitants) there are 92 churches. In 1999 a survey showed that more people go to church on a regular Sunday (175,000) than people who attend sports events. The question arises. Are Swedes really into sport?

- Swedes spend most of their lives in meetings. (Not at all. The writer of this book knows a lot of children and oldies who don't, but there is some truth to the statement.)

Moose

This big animal, called elk by the English, moose by the Americans, and älg by the Swedes, is referred to as the King of the Forest. 350,000 of these giant animals roam the forests until October, when they are reduced by approximately 100,000 during the hunting season (see Animal Life). During these hectic days teachers leave their schoolchildren, parents abandon their homes and the Swedish King takes off his crown, all with the intention of killing as many moose as they possibly can. Yes, there is a law to determine how many may be shot in a particular district. During this time tourists should refrain from picking berries in the forests. Hunters also hurt themselves — after drinking alcohol to keep warm, hunters have been known to shoot dogs, trees, other hunters and, although uncommon ... tourists.

On the roads in some parts of the country, one accident in three is caused by a moose landing on top of a car. If you are unlucky you might find yourself sitting in your vehicle covered in moose blood, intestines and steaks. Unfortunately many accidents involving them add to the statistics of motoring fatalities. (See Traffic!)

Music

Classical, jazz, folk or popular music are all represented in the Swedish flora of culture. For lovers of classical music "Drottningholmsmusik" by Vilhelm Pettersson-Berger could be recommended. For jazz lovers the mixture of jazz and folk music in Jan Johansson's "De sålde sina hemman" might be a good choice. As for folk music anything from the province of Dalarna is correct.

Abba, Roxette, Europe, Ace of Base, Secret Service, Blue Swede, Dr Alban, the Cardigans, Robyn, Swedish House Mafia, Avicii, First Aid Kit, Zara Larsson and Tove Lo, among many others, have achieved great success in the charts of pop music worldwide. Artists like Magnus Uggla, Tomas Ledin and Carola and so-called dance bands have sold 100,000s of records, if not millions, in Sweden.

Groups like Kent (not active anymore), Gyllene Tider and Roxette, plus artists like Zara Larsson, Tove Lo and Robyn represent the Swedish music phenomenon that placed Sweden among the best selling nations of popular music from the 90s (next to America and the UK).

Håkan Hellström, the golden boy from Gothenburg, sold out the large arena of Ullevi, with larger audiences than artists like Bruce Springsteen. Laleh, princess of pop, has a great following, just like Veronica Maggio with her enormous chart hits. Swedish groups and artists have to struggle hard to get to the charts, since the competition includes successful American and British artists and bands, as well as other acts from all over the world. Still, Swedish artists, bands, producers and songwriters have enjoyed a tremendous success over the years. Swedish House Mafia and Avicii (1989-2018) played a vital part in the House movement.

Muslims

There is an estimated number of half a million Muslims (unconfirmed) in Sweden. Fairly big mosques can be found in some of the major cities, whereas facilities in basements or block of flats or even industrial areas are being used in minor communities. "It is not important where we pray, as long as we have the opportunity," one Muslim said to the writer of this book.

People from the Middle East, Turkey and Iran have become successful musicians, writers, and journalists. Others are TV-personalities and doctors, nurses, shoemakers, restaurant owners, care assistants and IT-developers. Without them some institutions and work places would not function. Their contribution is necessary.

A problem, that has nothing to do with the categories described above, is criminality. No doubt, groups in cities, towns and smaller communities across the country have formed gangs and are involved in shootings, burning cars and selling drugs. Radical Muslims are trying to establish their territories and want other Muslims to refrain from taking part in Swedish elections. They also want to keep a tight watch on their younger members. Again, these people have nothing to do with the criminals above. The only common denominator is that both minorities create problems by refusing to obey Swedish law and to give in just a bit to the Swedish lifestyle. Of course, there are imams who dissociate themselves from the radical Muslims.

Myself

Once in a pool in Las Vegas, a Swedish tourist was approached by a truck driver who swam up to him, said "hi" and immediately started giving the visitor his life's story. Four minutes later it was time for goodbye and the bewildered Swede kept on swimming. The shocked tourist had met America at its best with its openness, its frankness and its directness.

In Sweden he had been taught not to emphasize himself or his importance, to know his place. He would have swum back and forth without speaking to anyone at all, had it not been for this American, his two divorces, heavy mortgage and sick old mother. The Swede might have interrupted him, although that is to be bad-mannered, and asked him about life as a truck driver. He is probably still swimming in that Las Vegas pool, unless he got up, dried and went to play the one-armed bandits on the Strip and won enough money to purchase a mansion in California – or a pool of his own.

Narcotics

Swedish subjects have been slow in catching up on this supernatural way of finding peace and happiness. Lately, however, the introduction has been sped up partly through good relations with the outside world. What belonged to the underground scene, through jazz- and rock musicians, now has invaded Swedish town squares, clubs, and schools. We tend to think this a growing problem. The efforts to stop drugs spreading all over, has been fought on many levels, but the attempt to defeat its dealers and users has not been successful. Still, Swedish policy is tough. A lenient attitude toward narcotics faces hard opposition in Sweden.

An adult male moose could weigh as much as 1,500 lbs, not a good road companion.

National Day

This holiday is observed in Sweden on June 6 every year. It took long to rename the Swedish Flag Day and make it into a national celebration. But today parades and flag-waving belong to this day. In Stockholm the royal family takes part in a ceremony at Skansen, the open-air museum. This is where little rosy children hand over bunches of flowers to the King and Queen while the blue and yellow Swedish flag is flying in the summer breeze.

Over the years a popular tradition has developed. New Swedish citizens are welcomed in ceremonies all over the country as they receive their certificates of citizenship in this heartwarming ceremony.

Nationalism

Swedes tend to regard themselves as not nationalistic. The only exception would be their love for the Swedish flag. Apart from that symbol, Swedish children are brought up with a feeling of belonging to the world and not a country. The goal of education is to foster caring and understanding world citizens and not chauvinist nationalists.

To speak in a patronizing way about immigrants is not tolerated publicly, but behind the scene another play goes on. "We are all equal and in this country we look after everyone, regardless of religion, ethnic groups, age or sexual disposition," could be said to be the official attitude in this nation of non-nationalists.

Swedes would never hold their right hand on the left side of their chest to salute the flag while singing the national anthem. That would be regarded as somewhat "too much." Sentimentality does not go with their image of not being nationalistic. "Lagom" should be "lagom."

The national anthem "Du gamla, du fria" ("Thou old and free") is often referred to as the "ice hockey song," played when a Swedish team has won the World/European Championship in a sport like ice hockey, swimming or handball. In that case sentimentality and nationalism are allowed. The only problem, it does not happen often.

[The] Swede

Swedes are obsessed with nature.

Nature

The Swedish population is obsessed with nature. In your contact with the natives you must observe the following rule: Listen patiently, nod as though you are interested and do not interrupt a Swedish subject going on and on about the beauty of his country. If you are invited to hike along a trail near the town or place where your host lives, do not put on boots and hiking gear. Swedes do not take it that seriously.

Neutrality

Sweden aims to stay out of alliances in peace time and maintain neutrality in war times. The country is surrounded by NATO neighbors but sticks to its own defense, which was reduced in number and financial means since the Iron Curtain and the Berlin Wall came tumbling down. Sweden has not been at war since 1814, when she attacked Norway and forced this friendly nation into forming a union, which lasted until 1905. By then the Norwegians had understandably had enough. Despite the lack of war, Swedish soldiers have been killed in international operations, like the ones in the Congo and Mali, the Middle East and Afghanistan.

News and weather on TV

The Swedish news on television differs from that of the English-speaking world insofar that it often includes a large portion of international news items and a smaller dose of domestic news.

The Swedes, who represent a country of only 10 million inhabitants, take great interest in global issues. Well-informed people should know about presidential elections in America, bushfires around Sydney, the Brexit situation, Scottish soccer and Canadian ice hockey. There are no guarantees, though. Still, American and British news in particular can be said to be part of the TV-world of Swedes.

The tempo in the news is slower than the very professional American well-oiled voices, spitting out lines like machine guns. Swedes simply like it at a slower pace, to have stories that are given more time. That goes for the weather report as well. For pedagogical reasons the Swedish method pays off better. You will remember the news and weather items, unless you have fallen asleep during the process.

Newspapers

In most major towns it is possible to buy international papers, and there are reading rooms in libraries where you can browse through them. If you have access to the internet, electronic editions of large newspapers are available. Ask at your hotel or in your host family.

No

If a Swede says "no" (nej or nä), it is often followed by a completely unnecessary explanation. "I have to go mushroom picking, I must paint my house tomorrow, I have to play with my grandchildren all day" or "I expect a cold to break out this coming weekend." You will rarely hear someone simply say: "No, I don't want to" or "No, I'm not interested." An immigrant working for the Social Authorities in a small town once said: "You must say either yes or no to my fellow-countrymen. They take "maybe" for a yes!"

The Swedish habit of leaving the door open to discussions might be regarded as plain weakness by new Swedes. To immigrants from other countries, where you can talk yourself into a better position, this Swedish attitude may be considered stupid. To Swedish natives it is a question of sheer politeness. Who wants a heated argument? Let´s keep it lagom.

Nobel Prize, the

Alfred Nobel (1833-1896), born in Stockholm, established the prize in 1895. By then he had made a fortune in his corporation Bofors. The chemist, inventor, industrialist, engineer and donor, held more than 300 patents, including dynamite.

The family owned oilfields in the Caspian Sea area, like in Baku, Azerbaijan. In 1888 Alfred's brother Ludvig died, and newspapers by mistake published an obituary for Alfred. He was called "the merchant of death." This triggered an inner fight. He decided to change this dynamite image into something good, and the Nobel Prize was born.

It is awarded for outstanding contributions for humanity in chemistry, literature, physics, medicine and peace. The Peace Prize ceremony takes place in Oslo. The reason is that between 1814 -1905 the two neighboring countries were in a union and it was only fair to give Norway some of the star quality.

Sixty-seven years after the first Nobel Prize awards, the Swedish Riksbank Prize in Economic Sciences in Memory of Alfred Nobel was established. Today it is regarded as a Nobel Prize, although technically speaking, it is not. It is also awarded in December with the other prizes in the Stockholm Town Hall in a lavish ceremony with exquisite food and musical performances in the presence of the Swedish royal family. Each prize recipient receives 9 million Swedish kronor (roughly $968,000, August 2019), along with a gold medal and diploma; the prize can be shared between up to three scientists which sometimes is the case in chemistry, physics and economics. An organization can also receive the prize which often happens with the Peace Prize.

Nordic companies

Sweden, being the largest Nordic country, holds seven places in the Nordic Top 10. Four banks, Volvo, Ericsson and Telia Company (telecommunications), make out the rest. H&M (retail in clothes) and Atlas Copco (capital goods) are in the Top 20.

Other large companies are Sandvik (capital goods), Skanska (construction), SKF and Electrolux (manufacturing). Vattenfall (energy), SCA (hygiene and forest products) and the ICA Group (food and health) are also successful corporations and make their way to the Top 10 in other surveys. IKEA is not included since it is registered and based in other countries.

Norrbotten

This province of the North stretches along the Swedish coast and the Finnish border. It offers beaches, large forests and good soil. Crofters, who started realizing the value of the forests, populated Tornedalen (Torne Valley) centuries ago. Industries and sawmills developed in the 19th and 20th centuries, and the port of Luleå was used for the shipping of ore from Lapland. In Boden, the old garrison town, the museum portrays its military history.

Haparanda, the border town in the east, developed when Sweden gave up the province of Österbotten to Finland after losing the Russian War. Piteå with Gammelstad (the old town with its unique 450 church cottages) and the famous sandy beaches are worth visiting. Storforsen, a natural waterfall in Piteälven (the Pite River), has several sights. A trip by car from Haparanda to Övertorneå and then Överkalix and back south will certainly impress any visitor.

Närke

The province of Närke, situated between Lake Hjälmaren (Sweden's fourth largest lake) and Lake Vättern (the second largest lake), was shaped by the thick ice that covered this part of the country until some 8,000 years ago. Kilsbergen, the so-called Blue Mountains, include lakes as well as fishing, hiking and skiing possibilities. Kvarntorp, east of Kumla, produced oil out of slate.

Närke also invites you to Wadköping, a picturesque part of Örebro. In the town centre of Örebro you will find the regional museum and one of the Vasa castles surrounded by a moat. Ekebergs herrgård (mansion) is the home of the beautiful white marble used for the interior of buildings. Askersund is a picturesque little town on Lake Vättern in the north, where the archipelago begins. It is worth visiting. Why not take a tour on a steamboat on Lake Vättern?

Old towns

In Australia or America an old town may be 100 years old. In Sweden it takes more to impress the natives. Sigtuna, with her 1,000 years of history or the former Viking town of Birka (8th century), might be called old. On the other hand, Birka does not exist anymore, only excavations reveal that it was there. Gothenburg, founded in 1621, will possibly be found in Division 3, which an Italian would call a "new" place.

The Swedes have made exactly the same mistake as the English by giving towns names like Nyköping (ny = new, köping = market town) or Nyhamn (= new harbor). For how long is a town new? Is New York new? Is York old?

Order

The Swedish longing for practical arrangements in about every aspect of life is clear in the desire to have everything measured. Doors, refrigerators, cupboards and carpets are of specific widths and heights to suit any home.

The Danish Lego system has similarities with the Swedish thinking. It enables the purchase of a new dishwasher or washing machine, where the exact hole left after the old one will match the new one. Standard measurements never fail. When you buy a condo or a house, a fully equipped kitchen, wardrobes and machines are part of the deal. So are the walls and floors.

Osvensk (un-Swedish)

"Unpopular," "unhappy" or "unsympathetic" all have a negative meaning and show discontent. The word "osvensk" (un-Swedish) on the other hand also displays admiration and fondness.

"The Texas cousin in his cowboy hat visiting relatives in Malmö," "the rowdy, cheering Scottish soccer fans at the UEFA-cup finals in Göteborg" or "the loud Aussies in their mid-20s at the Luleå pub" will all be regarded as "happy-go-lucky, charming foreigners." They will be accepted for what they are, nice, un-Swedish guests. Meanwhile the lagom Swedes will be wearing jeans, put on their scarves at the ice hockey game and speak in lagom-loud voices. We are now talking sober Swedes.

Page Three

If Swedish tabloids introduced pin-up girls on page 3, protests would be organized within hours. Political parties and their youth clubs, feminists, teachers, journalists, high school students and others would strongly oppose such a step backward to the Dark Ages. Individual males on the other hand might applaud such a nice addition to the evening paper.

Miss World and Miss Universe have also outplayed their role in modern society. To use a perfect body or face as a means to compete is regarded as old fashioned and unequal. To honor brains in a competition like the Nobel Prize though, is another story and widely praised.

Palme, Olof

He was born in 1927, the son of an upper class family in a wealthy part of Stockholm. After studying and traveling in the United States, he started a career in the Social Democrat Party and became its leader and Prime Minister of Sweden in 1969. He was a sharp, controversial figure with great importance in international politics.

Palme was a heavy critic of the Soviet Union, communist Czechoslovakia, Franco's Spain, fascist Portugal and South Africa with its Apartheid. He was the first western politician to visit Cuba, with a speech in Spanish, repeated later on in Nicaragua. On February 28, 1986, 20 minutes after 11 p.m., he was shot in a Stockholm street while walking through the city with his wife. In those days politicians did not have bodyguards 24/7. The murder has not been cleared up.

Parental leave

Mothers and fathers of newborn babies are entitled to take a total of 480 days off with 80% (to 90%) of their income. Fathers are encouraged to make use of their lawful right to stay at home. Parents are allowed to divide these months between them. If the father decides not to use any time whatsoever, he and his wife will lose 60 days due to this lack of interest.

Soon parents of 4- to 16-year-old children will be entitled to another three days a year per parent and child. Even a grandmother or a grandfather may stay home from work to help their daughter or son with their grandchildren. Then the parental leave—and the money—will be granted them instead, provided they have an income and are not retired.

Parties

Formal Sweden with her formal dress and manners passed away long ago. Today's parties are informal and "you don't have to be this or that way" in any respect. Simply be yourself.

Standing at a party is considered slightly funny. Of course you should be sitting on a sofa or in an armchair around a table, sipping a drink and making some conversation. Common topics may be taxes, school, infotainment, the latest sensational documentary on either SVT 1 or 2 or on the independent channel TV4. When the hostess calls, everyone is herded to a large table where, according to the Swedish equality system, they will decide which man will sit next to which woman. This may take a while.

Wine is served and the first sip is swallowed after a toast to life, the European Union, the royal family, the government or the landlady, depending on political belief or age. Then everyone in turn takes his or her share of the meat, the potatoes and the salad. Meanwhile, the hosts explain what ingredients have been used. They will not assist in carving meat or helping their guests. Any adult could handle the situation themselves. Expect chicken, fish or beef. Your empty dish will be left in front of you until everyone

[The] Swede

Osvensk, "un-Swedish," definitely a good thing.

has finished. Do not be surprised if the meal contains garlic. Swedes are said to eat more of this than even the Greeks. Smellaholics can be found all over the country, especially in major towns. After the dessert has been served, possibly with ice cream as the main ingredient, the guests will be transferred to the sofa again.

Do not expect them to talk all the time. Swedes need time to reflect and may be silent for a few seconds, minutes or hours now and then. Do not panic! This is natural behavior. Small talk was invented and developed in Britain or America. In Sweden this way of conversation is finally catching on.

Before leaving make sure you find the right shoes inside the entrance. You see, a great many natives still keep up the tradition of taking off their shoes inside. Others bring an extra pair for indoor use.

Apart from these remarks, an evening resembles any evening in the Anglo-Saxon world. You do not give a married woman red roses, you do not spit on the floor, you use the toilet for throwing up and you thank your hosts for a lovely evening.

A new phenomenon is slowly growing. The under-50s invite people, but the food is far from ready as they arrive. It may take an hour or two before you can fill your stomach. In the worst case, they expect you to take part in the cooking. "It is so natural and you talk to each other while behaving like a big family." So, dear guest, choose an older host or hostess—or a young one, depending on how hungry you are.

Permissiveness

The prejudice indicating that Swedes, especially young females, are promiscuous, is in most cases exaggerated. If you regard Italian Catholic youngsters or clean, Midwestern American teenagers as sexually permissive, then sure enough. Otherwise ordinary young Swedes, regardless of sex, try to stick to one partner at a time and have hopes of the future like everybody else.

Once an innocent Swedish girl on a language course in Torquay, England, bought a T-shirt with the words "every inch of a woman" printed on it. She asked her teacher why men all over the place whistled at her and made obscene gestures. That was her ticket to the world out of rural Sweden.

Personnummer

Swedish citizens have a unique combination of four numbers added to their birthdate, e.g. 640325-5019, which means that this man was born in 1964 on March 25. The last four numbers are worked out according to a sophisticated system, which only a professor of physics or a child would understand. The 1, being an odd number, indicates this is a man.

Pets

Dogs and cats top the charts. There are about 880,000 of the barking sort and more than 1,441,000 meowing animals in Sweden, farm cats excluded (2018). Believe it or not, parks and streets are lined with dog toilets. Gone are the days when a doggy bag had something to do with a restaurant. Today every owner is expected to pick up the little animal's stinking hot pile, put it (the pile) in a black plastic bag and throw it in the "letter box lookalike." These boxes are regularly emptied by park attendants. An alternative exists. Simply pick up the hot stinking pile, put it in your black bag, fasten it to the leash and keep on walking. Throw it away when nobody is watching you.

The horse has found its way into the hearts of families and in some communities there seem to be Icelandic horses or half- and full bloods in every field. All in all, there are 355,000 of them. Riding is a popular sport.

Rabbits, guinea pigs, hamsters, gerbils and rats are found in some homes. Budgies (parakeets) have a following too. Having an aquarium, where cichlids are the most popular species (personal opinion), because they take care of their spawn, herd them around the tank and protect them, is another hobby, especially among boys and men.

PISA results

Since 1997, the Program for International Student Assessment (PISA) is a worldwide study that evaluates education in various countries by measuring 15-year-old students' knowledge and skills in mathematics, science and reading. The test is repeated every three years (2000, 2003, 2006, 2009, 2012, 2015 and 2018 so far). Its aim is to compare countries and improve their education. For Sweden the development has been a sad road downward. Results have dropped in every test. In PISA 2015, in which 72 countries and 540,000 students took part, Sweden landed as shown below:

- Math - 24th place
- Science - 28th place
- Reading - 17th place

The Swedish political parties are struggling hard to find a solution to the problem, so far with some luck. The results are getting slightly better. The fact that parents and hard work could contribute to better achievements has been overlooked in the general debate it seems.

Pitch-accent language

In this group of languages, you will find Turkish, Japanese, Korean and Shanghainese and Norwegian. Swedish is another example. It has many two-syllable words where the acute and grave accents make them sound different.

In the first category you start low (acute accent) and climb higher when you pronounce the word and in the second you start high (grave accent) and go lower.

	acute accent	**grave accent**
biten:	the piece	bitten (by an animal ..)
kullen:	a litter of animals	the hill
skallen:	the barks (dog)	the skull

skotten:	the shots	the Scotsman
tomten:	the plot (of land)	Santa Claus

If you think this is complicated, then think about the 10 million that deal with this issue every day.

Polar bears

Let's get it straight: There are no polar bears in Sweden. Try Canada if you want a clear view of one or definitely Spitzbergen/Svalbard (Norway).

Polar Music Prize, the

This is a Swedish international award, founded in 1989 by legendary Stikkan Andersson (1931-1997), music publisher, manager of ABBA, songwriter and founder of Polar Music. He co-wrote songs with Björn Ulvaeus and Benny Andersson in the early days. The award is presented to one contemporary musician/group and one classical musician/choir or similar. It is "awarded for significant achievements in music and/or musical activity." It has been awarded to Paul McCartney, Quincy Jones, Elton John, Bruce Springsteen, Stevie Wonder, Bob Dylan, Burt Bacharach, B.B. King and Led Zeppelin. Other winners are Chuck Berry, Sting, Joni Mitchell, Grandmaster Flash and Paul Simon, just to mention a few.

Police

Dial 112 and you will be connected to the fire service, ambulance service or the police.

Swedish police officers are usually armed, carrying a pistol and a club. The profession has seen a growing number of students in their 20s wanting to enter the force. This in its turn means that competition is hard and that has led to a high standard in training as well as in formal education. With the equivalence of a university degree, the women and men in the force are well equipped for a tough job. The attempt to recruit police officers from ethnic groups has shown some signs of success.

The number of officers in the country can be described as too small according to authorities and researchers. Financial problems make it difficult to increase the number. Still, Sweden is said to be an average country in the EU as far as criminality is concerned. With the open borders that exist, criminal gangs from the former Soviet Union and the Balkans, just to mention two geographical parts, have found their way into Sweden. Swedish motorcycle gangs are well established too.

Politeness

The English way of expressing gratitude and being "polite" does not always apply in Sweden. "Thank you," "Sorry," "Excuse me, please" may be regarded as a bit too much sometimes. Not that anyone objects to these civilized manners, only that we run this business differently. Words do not necessarily mean everything. Gestures, nodding or a smile may substitute words. "Those silent Swedes" strike again in their kind way. However, do look under "tack" for more specifics on this subject.

After purchasing your red Dalahorse or moose T-shirt, the shop assistant cordially says, "Thank you." And that's it. No "Bye, bye" but possibly "Have a nice day" because they use that phrase a lot in American films and on television and Swedes want to imitate Big Brother.

Children are encouraged early on to express their feelings and their opinions. Do not think they are badly disciplined. They are supposed to be like that. You will probably find that these youngsters take part in conversations. Remember, they are not rude! They are Swedish.

[The] Swede

Sorry to disappoint: Polar bears are non-existent in Sweden.

Politics

Swedish politics should not be the subject at your first dinner party. Any other country or world politics will work just fine (like China, USA, Italy or Monaco) but when it comes to the nation's politics, most Swedes will keep their feelings to themselves. They are supposed to be very private. And please don´t call Sweden a socialist or communist country. People might get upset about your ignorance. It is no different from other Western democracies. There's a lot to talk about, however. Sweden is a multiparty system where eight parties are represented in the 349-member parliament, Riksdagen. They are usually grouped into blocks with the left consisting of Social Democrats (s, socialdemokraterna), The Green party (mp, miljöpartiet) and the Left party (v, vänsterpartiet) and the right, slightly more or even more conservative block consisting of the Moderate party (m, moderaterna), The Liberals (l, liberalerna), the Center party (c, centerpartiet) and the Christian Democrats (kd, kristdemokraterna). The Sweden Democrats (sd, sverigedemokraterna), which grew strongly over the last ten years based on a somewhat populist message, is shunned by the other blocks for being too radically against immigration. There were another twenty parties listed for the 2018 election but only one other national party, Feministic Initiative (fi, feministiskt initiativ) came close to the the 4% minimum of the vote to get a seat in parliament. They didn´t make it, but at least the Government has 10 women and 9 men (which may have changed slightly since the latest election), which is possibly a small relief but still. All in all, Riksdagen (Parliament) has 188 male members and 161 female members (the odd change may have occurred).

Poor country

Sweden may still be regarded as a welfare nation with a high standard of living and political stability. Still, if you go back to the 1860s, the country received aid from Europe in her struggle to survive. The situation resembled that in Ireland with failing potato crops, social injustice and famine. It was not until after the Second World War that her economy started to flourish. The expression "folkhemmet" (literally folk home,"we're all a big, loving family") was born.

To modern immigrants and refugees this fact may not always be known. Some new Swedes tend to think this wealthy state has always existed. They do not know about fairly poor households struggling to lead a good life even in the 1950s. Refrigerators, washing machines, one car per home, three bedrooms and closets filled with clothes, was all merely a dream for many Swedes as recently as 70 years ago.

Prehistoric Sweden and onward

Scandinavia became more or less ice-free around 11,500 BC. All ice had melted 6,500 years BC according to estimated calculations. Swedish nature today shows clear evidence of the ice's influence. It has left ridges, boulders, rocks and sand along its slow motion toward the south. As soon as the ice withdrew and melted, fishermen and hunters started moving in, often from the south of Sweden. The Sami population is believed to have come this way, then along the Norwegian coast but also from the east, via Russia and Finland. The Bronze Age began 3,500 years ago, followed by the Iron Age about 1,000 years later. The 9th and 10th centuries brought the Swedish Vikings who ventured far to the east, through what is Russia today, and westward (Danish and Norwegian Vikings) as far as America.

Prices

Germans, filling their vehicles to the roof with tins, packages, bottles of this and that and other food supplies, might give you the impression that Sweden is an expensive country. Instead it may only be a sign of these tourists' economic thinking, which is never wrong. Compared to other European countries or English-speaking nations all over the world, Sweden has normal prices, except for food, which is 20% more expensive. Clothing, entrance fees, travel and hotel prices are competitive with equivalent prices in America or Britain, sometimes lower. Prices should not discourage visitors, but come with an open heart and an open wallet. But, remember, conditions and prices vary. Check before you blame this writer for false information, please.

P-skiva

At parking lots in certain towns, the so-called p-skiva is used. It is rectangular and has something like a plastic or paper clock. After you park, set the time of arrival and display it in the front window. Usually you are allowed to park for free for two or three hours. Check the conditions before you leave your car. The p-skiva can be obtained in the town, at shopping malls and in certain stores. The best thing is to ask a nice local Swede about it.

Q-numbers

A queuing system that used to amaze foreign visitors has been in use for many years. Instead of choosing the wrong queue at the bank or the florist, you get a Q-number and then wait with the rest of the seemingly unorganized crowd until your number is displayed. Then you rush to the counter to get served.

If you happen to have 25 numbers ahead of you, rest assured that two or three people will get tired of all this waiting and leave. When their number is called and no one moves, the selfish, unashamed fellow-customers will jump the queue. They head for the salesman without producing their Q-number, in this way saving 10 minutes of queuing or more. Not one single customer will interfere, as they will be unwilling to take the risk of looking ridiculous in case they are wrong.

Raggare

This remnant from the 50s mainly exists in rural areas, in small towns and communities. These young men (raggare) drive big old American cars (raggarbilar). They are all Elvis Presley look-alikes and their rockabilly music invades the streets and the squares from their cruising automobiles. As a rule, everyone in the car, regardless of sex, will be drinking beer, except for the driver. The girls, however, have not kept that 50s look. They sit in the backseat or on the bodywork looking cool. Middle-aged Swedes may smile at them until they see the sign in the rear window: "Don't laugh. Your daughter may be in the backseat."

Rea

This word for "sale" can be found in various combinations. "Sommarrea," "januarirea" or "nattrea," are translated as "summer sale," "January sale" and "night sale." To make it easier for Swedes to understand they often use the word SALE, not REA.

Realtors

These distinguished members of society will not only sell a house and cheat you completely (not true), but they will also help you in anything that selling or buying a home means. The whole process—from showing you the property, house or flat, to studying the financial side, getting loans from your bank and explaining the contract—will be carried out by the Swedish realtors.

Today agents have a university degree of two years. That is supposed to make them even cleverer and able to find out how to get a better deal. 4–5% of the price will usually end up in the glove compartment of their Mercedes, but any fee may be discussed.

Recycling

Most Swedish homes recycle. First people fill their balcony, basement or kitchen with newspapers, cartons, tins, bottles and plastic material. Then they have an argument about the transport to one of the recycling stations. These are usually far out from the town center.

After deciding, they spill the last drops of their wine and strawberry jam in the trunk of their car. Then they drive to the local recycling station, where they go from one bin, full to the brim, to another one and select what to put where. Colored glass, non-colored glass, metallic objects, hard plastic material, soft plastic material, newspapers and batteries. In uncertain cases they look behind them and toss it into any container as swiftly as they are able to, and make a run for it. Mind you, the "garbage police" may see you! They do exist in the form of supervisors at the recycling station and are usually very cordial, to be frank.

If you prefer to throw away old furniture, cans of paint, old posters with plastic frames or the TV-set from the 90s, the same procedure starts all over again. Only this time you drive to another section of the recycling station. If it happens to be a Saturday, just follow the line of neighbors and old school friends until you get there. All these cheerful people may give you the impression that you have come to the motorway, but no! Wait for your turn, stop, talk to people, select the correct bin, talk some more, toss your old bicycle into the container and continue emptying your car and the trailer you rented from the gas station. An estate agent even proposed to set up a trailer and serve people coffee, in order to get potential customers. A month later—or more likely two or three—it is time for the same procedure again (not the coffee but the recycling). All this text about recycling has absolutely no importance to a foreign visitor. Neither has the rest. Sorry for the inconvenience.

Naturally you have at least two composts in your garden, which keep the little bugs inside them alive. Tea leaves, potato peelings, dead fish from your aquarium, and anything you can put in your mouth goes in there. While one is cooking the other has a rest period. It goes nice and squishy until you use the disgusting result the

[The] Swede

*The Swede is a fanatic when it comes to recycling.
It doesn't mean he's any better at it than anyone
else but it gets done, one way or another ...*

following summer. An option is to use the green and brown containers/barrels lent to you and collected by the local authorities every second week, at an annual fee.

Religion

Since the division of the Church and the State on January 1, 2000, a totally new situation has arisen. Now people are free to choose whether they want to stay within the Swedish Church, pay church tax or leave it. The Lutheran Church dominates totally, but a whole new church has arisen through a merger of the Swedish Mission Covenant Church, the Baptist Union and the United Methodist Church of Sweden. This new denomination is called Equmeniakyrkan (United Church of Sweden).

Churches of the Salvation Army, the Mormons, the Quakers and Jehovah's Witnesses all have thousands of members each.

Muslims have increased from practically nothing to hundreds of thousands in the last decades thanks to heavy immigration. Mosques can be seen in Stockholm, Göteborg and Trollhättan, to mention but a few places.

Roman Catholics play a certain role these days and have done so since the first Italians came in the 1950s. South Americans now increase their numbers.

The Orthodox Church is well represented through Poles, ex-Yugoslavians and people from former Soviet-Union republics and finally Greek immigrants.

Jews play a minor role in Sweden and have less than 20,000 members in their synagogues.

Approximately 3-4% of Swedes go to church on Sundays. This figure may appear low, but it exceeds the number of spectators going to sports arrangements on the same day.

If you're an American visiting Swedes, don't ask your hosts where their church is. They will look bewildered. Of course there are exceptions. Religion is not dead, only hidden.

Royal family

Since the Vasa dynasty (16th and 17th centuries), monarchy has played an important role in Sweden. The Bernadottes came to the throne after Sweden lost Finland to Russia in 1809. Through contacts in France, Napoleon's successful high officer Jean Baptiste Bernadotte was chosen for the Swedish throne. He accepted but his wife preferred to stay in France until she finally came to live in that backward, cold country with no culture whatsoever.

Conditions have changed since Gustav VI Adolf's days (1882–1973). He could be seen on his own in Stockholm streets in the 1960s, no guards, tipping his hat to subjects who greeted him. The current Swedish King, Carl XVI Gustaf, and his German-born Queen Silvia, have three children, Crown Princess Victoria, Princess Madeleine and Prince Carl Philip. There are also little princesses and princes charming the nation on occasions like baptisms and weddings.

The King, His Royal Highness, is addressed "the King" when spoken to. "Excuse me, has the King got any comment?" would be a direct question to him. Her Royal Majesty the Queen will consequently be addressed "the Queen." Young reporters have occasionally gotten carried away and used the friendly informal word "du" instead.

Our monarchy has a strong following according to surveys, and the royal family supplies media with enough material to fill page after page in the notorious "gossip magazines." In Parliament the number of monarchists and those in favor of a republic is more or less equal. The King's and prince's dyslexia, the Crown Princess's eating problems, and past boyfriends and girlfriends of the royal children never cease to interest hundreds of thousands of readers. In a comedy show they made jokes about Prince Carl Philip week after week, where he was portrayed as someone out of The Cuckoo Nest. Then he was invited to a show by his impersonator and immediately became everyone's hero. He was smart, funny, honest and a real comedian. After that we have heard no jokes about him.

Sami people

The Laps or Laplanders living in their territory named Sapmi prefer to be called Sami or the Sami people. Said to be the first settlers in the country, they live in the north particularly along the Norwegian border and inland.

Of the estimated 20,000–40,000 inhabitants (Sweden has no ethnic-based statistics), only 5,000 keep reindeer. The Sami people are a smaller group than for instance Kurds, Iranians, Britons, Americans, or Kosovo Albanians in Sweden. Their language, which is divided into three dialects, originates from the East (Europe and Asia) and cannot be understood by the average Swede. But it is one of Sweden's official languages. Today more Sami people live in Stockholm than in any other village, town or city.

Saturday night

In Britain young women can be seen on a Saturday night with no coats or jackets. Their bare shoulders glisten in the rain or in the cold winter night. Boys can be seen wearing shirts but no jackets. A young Swedish person going to a club or a concert would never dream of appearing half-naked. The simple fact is, it is too cold. Having been made to suffer warm comfortable houses with non-drafty windows, we have turned into big softies. It does not matter whether it is spring or autumn. We simply have to keep warm.

The English seem to stand the cold better than the Swedes. This phenomenon will be demonstrated every time a Swedish tourist stays in an English hotel or in a home. He or she will be cold or catch one. The good old British tradition of having a draft, supported by an open window, does not appeal to the natives of Sweden. They are not Vikings anymore!

School

Young Swedes start with preschool in many cases. At age 1 a child is guaranteed a place. At the age of 7, after preschool for one year, the majority enters their first year of the compulsory comprehensive school, where they spend nine years. But they do not leave this form of school for a never-ending freedom. Instead, the upper secondary school is waiting after their ninth summer holiday (early June to Mid-August) and another three years will be spent there. This applies to approximately 84% of the students who qualify for further studies. About 76% of these will graduate with a degree.

"What is the meaning of life?" This question shows the difficulty in explaining the Swedish school system. No one has succeeded yet. It is as complicated as life itself. In order to make this system even more complicated, authorities have developed the brilliant idea of changing it, say every five or 10 years, thus making it next to impossible to explain in a very unofficial guide book. In 2019 a new revised form of the grading system was officially announced.

The overall watchword is equality. If you take a vocational education you should have exactly the same possibilities as somebody in a natural science education of high academic standard. This leads to the conclusion that all students must study the same courses, doctors-to-be or mechanics, shop assistants or engineers. University has been designed for everyone, hasn't it? This is, however, not the complete truth. Each education has its own profile and courses too—at different levels of difficulty.

Grading does not commence until children reach puberty or are teenagers and ready to face it. By the time you read this text, grading may start as early as in the fourth year of school (aged 10-11). It goes from A-F, where A is the best grade. The Swedish school system changes constantly. This information may be out of date already.

The atmosphere in Swedish schools can be described as open, free, each one responsible for herself or himself. We trust our students. Too many rules restrict the possibilities to develop. Others would call the atmosphere chaotic. Students from an early age are encouraged to call teachers by their first name. (See Graduation day under "Studenten.") In normal cases the relationship between students and teachers in primary school (say years 1–5) and secondary school (years 6–9) means a lot of personal contact and care, although not to the same extent as in younger classes (years

1-5). There are however areas, where the atmosphere may not be described as one of harmony.

If you ask young Swedish students what their dreams look like, many will express their desire to become professional footballers, world-famous hip hop artists or simply people who make a lot of money, regardless of how to achieve this goal. The odd numbers may express a desire to become lawyers, vets or TV personalities. To obtain a better picture of the Swedish school system, consult the internet (Skolverket, Swedish Educational Board).

Security freaks

Swedes use bicycle helmets—the younger, the more common it is. Primary schools demand that they are worn. The reason is that far from all pupils get a lift by their parents to or from school and cycling on public roads can be hazardous. A majority of adults and children fasten their seatbelts while in the vehicle. They secure their stoves and ovens to avoid accidents involving their children. Swedes improve roads constantly and are only surpassed by the British in Europe as far as safety is concerned. Swedish children wear reflective badges on their clothes to avoid being run over in traffic.

Volvo, and at one time Saab, proudly improves safety in their cars all the time. The fire brigade inspects schools, and courses in first-aid are very popular. That Swedes use gloves while writing letters to avoid being smeared by toxic substances, might be somewhat exaggerated. That also goes for the rumor that Swedish toddlers wear crash helmets at home.

Sharing bedrooms

Swedish couples, engaged to get married, living together or those who simply have an established relationship are not allowed to share bedrooms when staying with relatives or friends in America. Is that still so or simply prejudice? How many young couples have not had this experience and found the somewhat prudish attitude remarkable? In their homeland no one would question their right to share a bedroom, even if suspicions may arise that they go to extremes and kiss each other in there.

Showers

The Swedish obsession of taking showers has existed for decades. Once upon a time, British hosts would marvel at the way Swedish kids on language courses had to take their numerous showers. First a bath, then a shower, was the ordinary routine. This was in the 1980s. The situation has changed and showers are part of our daily lives now, all over the Western world, right? The obsession lives on. One example is that students take showers after P.E. lessons, which in its turn means that they will be late for other lessons. The advantage is that they smell good.

Similar words with different meanings

Sometimes words may give you the impression that they are the same in the Swedish language. Mind you, they are not to be trusted all the time. Furthermore, their pronunciation also differs.

English versus the Swedish meaning of the words:

bad = swimming

den = it

fat = saucer

grind = gate

hem = home

is = ice

kind = cheek

mat = food

stick = beat it

tax = dachshund. Do you pay your tax? No, but I give him food.

Skåne

This is the province of plains and forests, soft ridges, beautiful fields and a long coastline. Agriculture dominates in this former Danish province, which in 1658 came into Swedish hands. Ale's stenar, stones shaped like a Viking ship, face the Baltic in the south. In the northwest another great sight, Kullaberg, invites guests to the lighthouse overlooking the water with a splendid view. This nature reserve attracts thousands of visitors every day.

In the north, Båstad with its tennis courts is close to Norrvikens Trädgårdar's famous garden. For hikers Söderåsen (Southern ridge) is the place to go. Österlen, an area on the east coast, offers sights of great beauty and harmony. This is where celebrities have summer houses.

Skåne has a large number of towns, including Malmö. A boat trip on its canals is popular. Parks, a castle, a modern library and lots of cozy cafés and restaurants make Malmö a good tourist resort. Other towns include Helsingborg with Kärnan, the old fortified tower, and Råå, a small fishing village, are all worth visiting. Twenty minutes by ferry from Helsingborg you are in Helsingör, Denmark. Lund, a pretty old university town, dates back 1,000 years. Another town, Landskrona with its citadel, has a ferry line to Ven, the lovely island.

Further to the south you can find Skanör-Falsterbo, the twin towns on the tip of a peninsula with lovely houses, sandy beaches and a golf course. Ystad (where crime hero Wallander acts), on the south coast, beats any town with its old houses. Continuing along the coast, the tourist will get to Simrishamn, a fishing port with narrow streets. Glimmingehus, a medieval castle, Kivik's market in July, the royal castle of Sofiero and the little place of Åhus are other sights there. Skåne is a tourist attraction in itself and should not be missed.

[The] Swede

Seeing all the bicycle helmets is not a sign that traffic is New York-like; it's all really a matter of common sense.

Slums

Slums do not exist in the sense that we have buildings ready to collapse with no heating, electricity or hot water. Some suburbs, though, have a large portion of new Swedes (immigrants) where conditions are not satisfactory. Mostly it is due to the fact that the newcomers are out of work or do not speak Swedish properly. These might be described as "mental slums." The percentage of unemployed Swedes in these areas aggravates the situation.

When an American journalist came to Sweden to report on the bad conditions of immigrants, he got the shock of his life. He believed in the myth of a socialist country that does not exist in reality and never has. It is as capitalistic as other neighboring countries. The suburbs were clean, housing standards very good, free schools were offered, social benefits were the same as for other citizens. Unemployment on the contrary was high.

Small talk

Two strangers meet.

1: "Two years ago I had a cold, really tough. Also, my car ran out of gas while I was touring the country. Then my wife died."

2: "Uhm, oh, yeah, bye."

To Swedes, small talk is no talk at all, it's nonsense. If you have to open your mouth to discuss the weather, someone else's children or the bus that is one minute late, then don't. The Swedes like to talk about real topics, like the weather, someone else's children or the bus that is one minute late. Honestly, we don't match the English or Americans' mastery of small talk. The good news is that even though it takes time to get to know us, we are friendly and sort of normal in the end.

Smoking

The number of smokers (rökare), applies to 7% of the population. Among teenagers the number of smokers has gone up with girls but is still low in an international comparison. On the whole girls seem to copy boys' habits, whether it is smoking or drinking. Sometimes Swedes pronounce the word "smoking" the English way. They then refer to black tie dinner jackets, but the word should actually have an "å" sound instead (like in the word "law").

Småland

Hard working crofters have piled up rocks and stones all over this province in the south neighboring Skåne. It's everlasting evidence of generations of slaving farmers. Plenty of nations like Finland and France produce beautiful glass these days. Still, the glassworks in the province of Småland draw crowds of people. It is an opportunity for the visitor to see products being made and buy them. Småland is the province where Astrid Lindgren was born and in Vimmerby there is a fantastic adventure park for the whole family with her figures. Kalmar, with its old castle and the spectacular bridge leading to the Isle of Öland, attracts thousands of tourists every summer.

Småland stretches from the pretty archipelago in the east along the Baltic. It continues along the beautiful coastline, from Kalmar across the large forests to Jönköping or from Tranås in the north to Växjö and its university in the south, there is so much to see.

Eksjö with its old wood houses, Blå Jungfrun (an island) with a national park, Gränna on Lake Vättern and the ferry boat to the Isle of Visingsö, Jönköping with its more than 700 years of history, Stensjö by (18th century village), Västervik with its picturesque wooden houses and places like Vimmerby, Vetlanda and Pataholm are other examples of sights worth taking a look at.

Smörgås

When you eat a slice of bread, spread butter on it. Don't expect your own personal knife next to your plate, forget it! There is one—and only one—for everybody. After all, we are a bunch of socialists.

Then use the cheese slicer and add a thick layer of hard cheese bearing names like "herrgård" (mansion), "präst" (priest) or "hushållsost" (household cheese). Get a good grip on the bread by using your thumb on one side and the other fingers on the other side of the bread. Lift it, bring it to your mouth. The rest you will have to work out for yourself. Do not attempt to break your slice of bread into two. That might be considered "foreign" or even osvenskt. (See Osvensk!)

If you prefer continental or white bread, stick to it. You might, however, try the Swedish "sweet" bread, which as the name implies contains sugar. Mind you, it is different. Tunnbröd (thinbread) from the north and hönökaka (round flat bread) from the west are two specialties worth trying.

Smörgåsbord

To most Swedes this means a large variety of foods served on a long table, where you pick whatever you wish to have. Typically at Christmas, Easter or any other special occasion, such as being on a Stena ferry to Germany, it is essentially a luxurious buffet with lots of seafood.

You should start with the seafood. If you are in a restaurant, do not hesitate to use a new plate for each helping. In a private home look discreetly at other guests first or simply ask. Fish dishes usually have herring as the main ingredient. There will be this fish prepared in any way possible, in mustard sauce, in plenty of onion or loaded with spices. Go easy on it! Salmon and "Jansson's temptation" (layers of potato and anchovy and cream, baked in the oven and served in an oblong dish) are generally included.

After seafood comes the meat. If you end up at a Christmas smörgåsbord, there will be plenty of ham. Half of it will be pre-sliced for the convenience of the guests. Do not faint at the sight of a pig's head with an apple in its mouth. The good news is that this disgusting habit is never practiced in homes, at least not to the same terrifying extent as earlier.

"Prince sausages" (short sausages), meatballs (minced meat made into balls the size of a small bird's egg), omelettes and patés make an appearance on any self-respecting smörgåsbord. At Christmas, another two specialties must be added: "dopp i grytan" and "lutfisk." They are not to be recommended to a first-time visitor.

The first dish above (dopp i grytan) consists of the fat being left after the cooking of the ham. Added to this is "vörtbröd," a spicy Christmas bread. You dip a slice of bread into the hot "broth," put it on your plate, add apple cheese (mashed apples) on top and eat the somewhat gooey bread. Lutfisk has been kept in the open for months to be absolutely dried. By the time Christmas gets closer a hunk of this white fish is placed in water to be softened up. You eat it with egg sauce and add lots of pepper to it. Boiled potatoes belong to this favorite dish. Mix it all and start enjoying this Christmas dish.

To quench your thirst after the herring and "Jansson's temptation," try a lot of beer or other suitable beverages. Wine is not usually served with a smörgåsbord. Schnapps on the other hand will be downed after the unavoidable singing. "Helan Går" or "Let's take it now, let's take it now. (slurp) We took it now" and similar little jingles.

The trick you should adopt at a smörgåsbord is to try as many dishes as possible without overdoing the amount. Do not attempt to fill your plate with one dish. Otherwise you may have to refrain from another helping because you are full. And your favorite dish may be among those.

Smörgåstårta

It looks like an ordinary birthday cake, with the exception that the smörgåstårta contains various rather thin layers of bread. Between each layer there is mayonnaise or a similar filling. On top of the cake you will find slices of salmon, ham or turkey, maybe a number of prawns, lettuce, tomatoes, cucumber and exotic fruits. Its contents vary from cake to cake.

The smörgåstårta looks not only appetizing but also beautiful, at least until the first guests have cut a few pieces of it. Then it collapses and at the end there are bits and pieces all over the plate. The "landgång" (sailors' gangway) is a variation of smörgåstårta, in a rectangular shape and in different sizes.

Snus

A South-African translator who had come to work for a Swedish company finally approached her boss and shyly asked: "Excuse me, but why have you got this bulging side on your upper lip sometimes? Is it some kind of disease?" The managing director showed her his round box with the letters "snus" (snuff) on it, opened it and asked her to try it. She backed off in dismay. That was her first lesson in "snus."

In the second lesson he took a grip on the dark brown mud in the box, made it into a ball with his fingers, opened his mouth and placed it under his upper lip. He explained that men use snuff instead of tobacco. Sportsmen seem to prefer it to smoking. Older teenagers probably find it manly. Women who use snuff buy it in something like small teabags. Don't always blame the parents for their child's looks. They were not born like that.

Sommarstuga

To own a summerhouse on a rocky island in the province of Bohuslän or along the Baltic coast will remain a dream to Swedes. Thousands already possess a cottage here, which means a sane investment and many pleasant days in the sun. Others prefer to purchase a cottage inland—often to simply keep busy with constant renovation projects.

For skiing families a cottage in one of the many skiing resorts in the north has high priority. For people with no possibility to buy a summerhouse, renting one can be an expensive but suitable road to pursue. A holiday in southern Europe may be another alternative.

Songwriters

Charts all over the world, such as the American Billboard and the UK charts and most other charts worldwide, have been invaded by Swedish music, written by producers, DJs and musicians in a never ending flow of inspiration. Benny Andersson and Björn Ulvaeus of ABBA, still make millions of dollars a year.

Denniz Pop (1963-1998) introduced a new kind of songs in his Cheiron studio. Since his death the most successful individual is no doubt Max Martin, sometimes co-working with Shellback. Other winners are Rami Yacoub, Ali Payami, Alesso, Avicii and Peter Svensson (former member of the Cardigans).

Axwell, Sebastian Ingrosso and Steve Angello, former Swedish House Mafia, have also contributed to the overwhelming results of Swedish popular music. Artists like Britney Spears, Taylor Swift, Ariana Grande, Justin Timberlake, Kate Perry, Pink, Kelly Clarkson and Backstreet Boys have sung songs written by the Swedish crème de la crème.

Snus. Banned in Europe but omnipresent in Sweden.

Spanking

For decades, spanking or punishing a child, in other words using physical force has been prohibited by law. Rare cases of children going to court in order to have one parent convicted for hitting them are known. Pocket money seems to have risen heavily during the same period of time. A connection may be suspected. A poor foreigner boxed his son's ears in Stockholm. He was sent to court.

Despite this limitation in correcting a child, they grow up and become mature citizens. "A little non-spanking doesn't hurt!" as the saying might go.

Speaking English

There will be no difficulties using your Texas accent, the Queen's English or even Aussie lingo, and who knows you might even be understood. The natives love to speak English, which is a compulsory language for all children in Swedish schools.

They start at an early age and mostly continue until they leave school at the age of 19. You will have to remember though, that they have worked hard to master English the way they do. Try to learn a couple Swedish phrases and you will understand why you ought to be slightly humble in your conversation with them.

There are a great many Anglo-Saxon films. Most of these films and TV programs have subtitles. This means Swedes who switch on the TV will probably have to listen to an American cop, a New Zealand farmer, an Aussie shepherd or an Irish emigrant setting off for New York, though not always in that order. The odds that an American president appears are high.

Sport

A large variety of sports attract sportsmen and women all over Sweden. Generally speaking, football (soccer) and ice hockey draw the largest number of viewers on TV. As for active players, football far exceeds those of ice hockey, but in popularity they tend to share the first place in the Swedish world of sports.

Handball has taken Sweden to the top of international competitions on a great many occasions and has a large following from a local to an international level. Bandy, played on ice the size of a football field (it seems) with two teams, is another winter sport. Armed with curved clubs and a hard "tennis ball" the swift players try to hit the ball into the huge goal where the poor goalie—without a club—has to defend it. Floorball (inomhusbandy) has spread like wildfire. It is played indoors. Two teams with curved clubs try to get the small ball into an equally tiny goal. The game is fast and furious and new clubs (Got it?) are emerging all the time. Some would call this indoor hockey with an air ball.

Tennis, basketball, skiing, martial arts and riding, among other sports are very popular in Sweden.

Spotify

It is a music streaming service, launched in 2008 in Stockholm. Daniel Ek and Martin Lorentzon introduced the company on the New York Stock Exchange in 2018, when they were estimated to have more than 180 million active users, more than half of them paying subscribers. Spotify pays royalties to artists and bands based on streams. The compensation has been criticized for being too low but if an artist gets one million streams that will surely generate a lot of money. For newcomers this is a good way of being heard and getting started.

State, the welfare

Sweden had the advantage of not participating in the two world wars. Consequently the country was able to create a welfare state, something now copied and modified in countries in the Western world. She had time to integrate women into her industry and offices. The National Health Service system was born after the Second World War at the same time Sweden shot to the top position among the Top 10 wealthy nations.

The standard of living was created in a melting pot where extensive welfare benefits and a full-scaled system of capitalism met and thrived. Over the last two decades or so, Sweden has seen a certain decline or rather other countries have caught up and in many cases overtaken her social reforms. The country has slowly but surely faced recession and has dropped down a few positions in the economy and welfare league. This came as a bit of a shock to the Swedes who tended to see their country as the place everyone would want to live in. Sweden is still a successful, prosperous country, though.

A Malaysian businessman on a visit to Sweden expressed his amazement at seeing the Swedish managing director, whom he was to have a meeting with, at the airport. "Are you so poor in Sweden that you cannot afford a chauffeur!" he said on their way to the office in Mr. Svensson's Porsche.

Stavgång

Do not be alarmed if you see older people walking with long sticks—but no skis. This kind of exercise supposedly does your heart good and will make a lot of muscles that you did not know you had work hard. Sometimes you may see groups of people briskly coming down a path in the park or in the woods.

Staying in somebody's home

"Guests, like fish, begin to smell after three days." This old saying, allegedly coined by Benjamin Franklin, was once uttered by an American relative to his host family in Stockholm. He stayed another week.

Staying in a Swedish home has got nothing to do with this rather funny statement. Swedes usually entertain their guests well. After a typical Swedish breakfast, sightseeing begins. A trip to the town or city center, to the coast, to an island, to the forest nearby or to some other well-known sight will probably be included in the program. Do not expect lunch or dinner in a restaurant. This is not a Swedish custom. For most hosts and hostesses that would be too costly. Besides, it is a lot nicer to find a lake where you can place a picnic basket on the ground and eat sandwiches, hot coffee and in many cases cinnamon buns and take in the beautiful surroundings.

Entrance fees and such will be paid for as will the ice cream eaten by you and your host family while you are all looking at the beautiful scenery or the busy street.

After you have returned to the apartment or house, dinner will be served. Chicken, beef or fish may be on the menu, unless you have clearly stated that you are a vegetarian or dislike fish. After coffee, small talk begins. In the early evening another tour may start, if it is the summer season. A local trip in the family car may show you what a Swedish town or place looks like.

Tea or coffee with a pile of sandwiches may very well be on the table later in the evening. Swedes tend to eat the main meal at lunch or in the afternoon. With guests, this habit may change. The odd TV program in English can be watched, and by the time you start yawning the host will give you an offer to withdraw or stay with them for another hour or two. You may be offered a drink or some fruit.

Stockholm

This city, the Venice of the North, must be treated as the absolute number one choice for foreign tourists. The rest of the country can be seen after they have been to Stockholm.

The unique island, which constitutes the original town of Stockholm, always thrills guests, even the Germans who have their beautiful old Hanseatic towns. To spend a day in the neatly laid out Gamla Stan (Old Town) with its maze of alleys and houses from the 17th and 18th centuries is compulsory for any tourist. If you visit the Royal Castle, do not expect to see the king and queen, as they decided that pollution was too much for their children. That is why the family now resides at Drottningholm (castle), not far from Stockholm. The sad thing is that their children have grown up and left. As the royal anthem goes: "Wherever I lay my crown, that's home."

The central parts of the city offer shops, department stores, restaurants and cafés in abundance. Hötorget (Haymarket), Kungsgatan, Drottninggatan and Sergels Torg with Kulturhuset (House of Culture) are streets or squares where you will end up sooner or later. Kungsträdgården with its benches, fountains, trees and cafés will calm you down and give your feet some rest. You may look at the Opera House from the lower part of the park.

Djurgården (Animal Farm!) is a large island with a zoo and old traditional houses in an open-air museum (Skansen), an amusement park and Valdemar's Udde (the art museum of Prince Eugen's paintings). North of Djurgården, Kaknästornet (a tower) would have given you a splendid view of Stockholm from a height of about 150 meters, if it hadn´t been closed due to the terror risk.

Riddarholmen (Island of Knights) with its church from the 13th century, the palace belonging to the Wrangels and Birger Jarl's Tower will appeal to your sense of imagination. People lived, loved and died here 700 years ago. Stadshuset (City Hall), on the other side of the water, looks like a church. In fact it is a city hall where the Nobel festivities take place. It has a registry office room for (non-religious) weddings.

Söder (South), the island south of the Old Town, with its many streets and small shops, includes parks and old houses. The T-bana (underground/ subway/metro) takes you around Stockholm, unless you prefer to go by bus to get a better view. Tourist cards exist, as they do in most big cities, with a price reduction on local transport and entrance fees. You have a large choice of museums, like National Museum with its paintings, Moderna Museet with its modern art, Millesgården with its huge statues by the artist Carl Milles. Also here is another highlight, Vasamuseet, with the spectacular ship from the 17th century which sank on its maiden voyage.

Stockholm, I'm from (I'm from Göteborg)

Anyone from Solna, Nacka, Haninge, Huddinge, Värmdölandet or Upplands Väsby appears to think that they come from Stockholm. It is like saying that someone from La Jolla or San Bernardino comes from LA. In this way they show that they are proud of the royal capital and want to be part of it.

As for Gothenburgers, they think differently. They really say that they come from Kungälv, Lerum or Särö and not from their neighboring big brother Göteborg. It is unclear whether this is out of pride for their local town or the shame of coming from the Gate to the West. Apart from this, Stockholmers and Gothenburgers are hospitable and easy-going city people. Do not hesitate to ask them for the bus station or the tourist office. You will need their assistance.

Stores

The British system of keeping the old grocers, fishmongers, florists and butchers is a charming way of encouraging customers to do their daily rounds, according to Swedes. That is why it was abandoned in Sweden decades ago. It did not match their need for practical thinking. Supermarkets and malls have replaced them in major towns and cities. You go to one place once a week, preferably

Stavgång.

on a busy Friday afternoon or Saturday morning when everyone else, including retired citizens who have all the time in the world, make their purchases.

The truth, however, is that there are smaller shops of times gone, where you buy flowers, hardware products, shoes or whatever. A lot of this has been made possible thanks to new Swedes. They have their own businesses like the way things once were. Convenience stores are often run by these immigrants, who also dominate in kebab- and pizza places. They are well represented as shoemakers too.

The plastic or paper grocery bags that you pay for at the supermarket check-out have got handles, thus enabling you to carry more than one at a time. In Britain they have handles too, but you do not pay for them. In Sweden they are being phased out (since around 2017) and people are encouraged not to use them. Bring your own when you go shopping!

Strindberg, August

Strindberg (1849–1912) wrote novels and plays that have affected a lot of Swedes in one way or another. His "Hemsöborna," where he describes life on an island, is a landmark. "The Red Room" with its realism was the first modern novel in Sweden, "Miss Julie," the passionate drama between a butler and his mistress is another, and "A Dream Play" (an expressionistic drama) another success. You can never be neutral when it comes to reading his works or see them at the theater. Strindberg awakens your mind. His novels and plays have been translated into English.

Studenten

To graduate from upper secondary school (after 12 years at school) is called "ta studenten." This happens in early June all over the country. The traditional ball usually takes place in advance of graduation day.

On the last day of school, celebrations in most schools start outdoors, where champagne breakfasts are served. The traditional white hat is put on and female students will mainly be dressed in white whereas male students often wear tuxedos or dark suits. This final day is spent with classmates and the school master or mistress. After the common handing over of presents to the beloved teachers, who are even more popular on this day due to the students' consumption of alcohol and possibly sentimentality, speeches are held and everyone signs each other's hats.

Eventually the assembly hall receives students by the hundreds, making it look like a lake of swans, as one principal put it. In a nice atmosphere solemn music is played, mixed with traditional summer songs. Speeches are made, cheers, noise, sounds and laughter fill the hall. In the schoolyard family and friends cover the "newly baked students" (as the expression goes) in flowers around their necks and objects like walking sticks, teddy bears or dolls. Students leave their school (for the last time) in decorated floats. These may vary from tractors covered in green branches of birch trees to sports cars and big trucks. In many small towns all these vehicles make a procession. There will be excessive singing and shouting. The odd drop of alcohol also contributes with its effects.

At home aunts, uncles, grandparents, neighbors and friends continue the party. Maybe they have a large smörgåsbord or some other kind of buffet. Gifts will be handed to the student in his or her white hat. In the evening students have parties, while families celebrate the "invisible guest of honor." Traditions vary from school to school, from place to place.

Stuga

It means "cottage" or "small house." You will see "stuga" printed or handwritten on signs in the countryside. It refers to a vacant stuga nearby. Often you will find the text "300 metres" or something similar, which tells you how far away the stuga is. Prices are reasonably cheap. Airbnb is another option.

Suck it, baby

The French couple was invited for a nice evening in a Swedish home. They probably expected beef or chicken or fish of some kind. But they were in for a surprise. The hostess had prepared a Swedish specialty—shellfish of all kinds. The poor French guests started eating prawn by using forks and knives.

Meanwhile the primitive Swedes broke their necks (those of the prawn), peeled off the shell and swallowed the tail. They proceeded by sucking the claws and interior parts of the crayfish, making absurd noises. By then the French visitors were no doubt longing for their charming escargots. Next time, if ever they come back, they will hopefully not be offered surströmming (see below).

Surströmming

This delicacy of the north will come up as a topic when you speak to the natives of Sweden. Everyone will pretend to have eaten this fermented herring, but most of them have better taste than that.

This fish from the Baltic will be kept for months in barrels. It is transferred to cans and by the time it is so well fermented that the top of the can bulges, the feast can start. This happens in August and September.

Here follows a true story. The table was beautifully laid in the garden. Onion and "mandelpotatis," which is a special kind of fingerling potatoes growing in the north, and "tunnbröd" (thinbread) were waiting to be eaten. The caring father who'd relocated to the Göteborg area took his little daughter in her pram to the nearest park, opened the can carefully and got the exploding fluid all over himself. He then proceeded home with pram and child, presented the dish to wife and children, and three minutes later took it back to the park and threw it away. Meanwhile the neighbor exclaimed while closing her window: "Rotten fish smells terrible. I can't stand those Northerners and their disgusting traditions!" At the same time the surströmming lover's wife concluded, "I didn't know it was that bad. Go and get the burgers, children!"

Svensktoppen

This popular radio show started in the early 1960s and has become an important factor in the Swedish version of country music, light pop and "dance music." Some of the music reflected in the program is aimed at ballrooms where people still dance and hold each other tight. Up-tempo tunes also play a role. Songs that have been written for the Eurovision Song Contest regularly appear in the show, often successfully.

The listeners range in age from 20 to those in their 80s or 90s. Either you are pro-Svensktoppen or you are anti-Svensktoppen. Quality is a matter of opinion. If you want to hear the same 10 songs month after month, this is the program. Not much happens. The good news is that you may learn Swedish that way or if you want to improve your English that is also possible. Both languages are accepted today.

Svensson

To most Swedes "Average Svensson" is a synonym of a Swede, like average Joe in the USA. Today the name only holds the number ninth position in the Top Ten of common names. When Sweden went from left-hand driving to right-hand driving in 1967 there was even a song played all the time wherever you went. It was called "Håll dig till höger, Svensson", literally meaning "Keep to the right, Svensson".

Here follows a list of ten Svenssons, not necessary the most well-known ones but at least representatives of different aspects of life.

- Alf Svensson (leader of the Christian party for 31 years)
- Amanda Svensson (modern writer)
- Emma Svensson (popular photographer)
- Esbjörn Svensson (jazz musician, 1964 – 2008, died in a sports accident)
- Gloria Swanson (American actress, her ancestors, the Svenssons, originated from the province of Småland)

- Kalle Svensson (legendary football goalie)
- Klara Svensson (boxer, 63 kg)
- Lill-Babs Svensson (Barbro, 1938-2018, a giant in popular music and chansons)
- Paul Svensson (TV-chef, cookbook writer)
- Pål Svensson (sculptor, represented all over the world)

SWEA

This acronym stands for Swedish Women's Educational Association. It is a non-profit organization for Swedish-speaking women abroad, founded in LA. It supports Swedes living abroad, awards scholarships on an annual basis, cooperates with Swedish businesses, and assists our Foreign Ministry in emergency crises. The Swede of the Year award is given to women, like the Queen, opera singers and famous female chefs, among others.

Swear words

Swear words are not as diversified in Sweden as in most Western countries. Religious and possibly anal words are used. That's it! Due to contact with the outer world and new Swedes we are picking up the odd, strange swear words though. We have to thank the Anglo-Saxon world for all the new f*-words and the mother*-word.

Sweden best country in the world

"We're not as good as we think. Remember the burning cars, criminals shooting each other, the low wages of nurses and the problems in our schools. And we have politicians only caring for themselves."

Well, maybe Swedes should think again and be more proud of their country. In various surveys as to what countries are good at, Sweden always hits one of the best spots. In Business Insider Nordic, Sweden comes in at #1, followed by Denmark, Norway and Finland in that order and the 9th position goes to Iceland.

In U.S. News & World Report Sweden can be found in 6th place after Switzerland, Canada, Germany, UK and Japan. The country is in the Top 10 for: business-friendly, cultural influence, most modern entrepreneurship, quality of life, raising kids, green living, retiring comfortably and women. (CNBC.com)

Cntraveler.com points out certain aspects of life where Sweden is far ahead of most nations like: style & beauty, pop music, green living, work-life balance, culture and gender equality.

When Petter Stordalen, the Norwegian hotel billionaire, praises us, people look surprised, thinking, "Are we that good?" Maybe we are.

Surströmming.

Swedes pronouncing English words

The Swedish shurdy gurdy sound does not resemble the sound of the English language. This constitutes a problem for most Swedes, unless they have been au pairs abroad for a year or have been seduced and lured into marriage by some Californian or New Yorker.

For a trained ear there are different accents, which divide Swedish English into: Stockholm English, Gothenburg English, Scania English and Northern English, just to mention a few.

As for the English vocabulary, some sounds are difficult to imitate—or people simply forget to articulate or they show a careless attitude toward the pronunciation of the English language. That is why you will hear phrases like: in Yune Yohn and Yane will go to Yohannesburg or the yungle. If someone's American cousin went to Yale or jail is difficult to tell. And a yoke is a yoke or a yolk. Sometimes thirty will be tirty and a thousand a tousand. Sharlie might shoose sheddar and not shocolate.

To our defense, it must be said that even thousands of Irish English speaking citizens have copied our charming pronunciation as far as the "th-sound" goes—or is it vice versa? Occasionally you may hear somebody "eating fish 'n' ships" and others "putting on their new leather boats." On the whole though, communication will work. Even people in their 70s or 80s may impress you by answering in English.

Swedish Sin

The Swedish sin has been an international concept since the early 1950s, created by such films as "One Summer of Happiness" or Ingmar Bergman's "Summer with Monika" which feature a great deal of nudity. In 1960, the U.S. president Eisenhower used Sweden as an example of the dangers of socialism, stating that the welfare state had led Sweden into an orgy of "sin, nudity, drunkenness and suicide." In reality Swedes are no different from other nations but do possess a relaxed, some would say more natural, relationship with skin and nude bodies. The country was also first in the world with compulsory sexual education (1955) but do not expect Swedes to be more open to sexual relationships than any other nationality. In "what a pity" and "what a sin" the words "pity" and "sin" are the same (synd) in writing and pronunciation. Is that a coincidence?

Swimming

When you choose a spot on the beach for your family or friends, try not to upset people by using the "foreign occupation trick." You don't need half the space of Europe for a picnic. If you spread towels, shoes, bags and children's toys all over the place to indicate to the world that you have occupied the marked area, you will not be liked. Muttering voices will accompany you all day.

On the whole, it is wise not to speak too loud. Loud foreign guests give a bad impression. Swedes, though, may shout to their kids. We are all equals, but some are more equal than others (quote from Animal Farm, G. Orwell).

Whether you have come to a lake or the Baltic, do not make too much fuss when the time has come for you to get undressed. No sneaking behind bushes is necessary. The Swedes do not show any sign of shyness, but are discreet. No one exposes his or her body to other people on the beach. Using "garden sheds" or "bus stop shelters" on the beach belongs to other nations, where everything will have to be handled so that nobody sees breasts or behinds in their natural habitat. By the way, most children learn to swim in school or in swimming courses.

As for getting into the water, no matter how cold it may be, look as though you are enjoying every second of it. To find out what temperature the water holds, a man may discretely look inside his swimming trunks. One centimeter means very cold, two centimeters pretty cold. Enjoy.

Systembolaget

Feel like a bottle of wine? Try the local supermarket and the next and the next. The chances of finding alcoholic beverages are as small as spotting a tiger in the Old Town of Stockholm. Instead look for the sign "Systembolaget." This is a national state-owned chain of shops where you will find a varied assortment of alcohol—and nothing else.

No, this is not a joke, I repeat, no joke. Governments of yesteryear decided to steer this business centrally. In smaller places without Systembolaget you can order spirits at the local store or any other appointed store. The postman will deliver it there, and an employee will hand it over in your shaky hands, looking envious. A complicated operation, yes, but it works and your consumption of alcoholic beverages will automatically decrease.

The company encourages its customers to refrain from drinking. Hence they advertise, informing the citizens what effects alcohol has on your body and what the risks are. They are probably the only company in the world trying to go bankrupt. "Do not buy our products. They may damage your health!"

Södermanland

This province has an abundance of relics, churches, graves and other objects from prehistoric days. Rune stones and medieval churches are other trademarks of Södermanland, as are the waterways between the Baltic and Lake Mälaren. Mansions and castles appear all over this part of the country.

The province, to the west and south of Stockholm (the southern parts of Stockholm are in Södermanland), ranges from the Baltic Sea with Nynäshamn and the ferries to the Isle of Gotland to Mariefred and Gripsholm (Vasa) Castle with its thick walls. Dalarö, the small summer resort overlooking the archipelago, has unique qualities as a place of peace and beauty, just like posh Saltsjöbaden. Anyone interested in agriculture or forestry should visit the Museum of Agriculture at Julita, a mansion owned by the Nordic Museum. Trosa, a small town called "the end of the world," was burned by the Russians in 1719 but emerged again. The word means "knickers/underwear" in modern Swedish. The original meaning is believed to have to do with the word mouth (of the river).

Eskilstuna attracts tourists with its zoo and several museums. Nyköping (13th century) with the notorious royal killings in the castle offers interesting finds from that period. Strängnäs consists of narrow streets with low red houses and its history goes back to the 12th century. Torshälla, this place of worship where Thor, the god, was worshipped, already existed in the days of the Vikings.

Taciturn Northeners

Two woodchoppers, Bengt Marklund and Ivar Nordström, are having a party. Bengt says: "Hey, Ivar!" Two weeks later Ivar hits Bengt in the face. Another week later Bengt asks: "Why did you do that?!" Another two weeks and the answer follows: "You talk too much!" This story seems to reflect some kind of prejudice of the 87% of Swedes who look upon the 13% living in the northernmost provinces as quiet, grave fellow countrymen living in eternal darkness and fifteen feet of snow.

A word of advice: Talk to people up there, if ever you get as far north as the nine northernmost provinces. It is worth a trip. You will see trees, trees, trees and possibly more trees apart from lakes and lakes. Breathtaking, peaceful, quiet and irresistible!

Tack

Although Swedes are not generally as adapt at being polite and gracious as our Anglo-Saxon cousins, the word "tack" will come up automatically under a lot of different circumstances. "Tack för maten", literally "thank you for the food" is said after a meal and has been ingrained in every Swede from childhood, as has "tack för senast", "thanks for the last time" - usually used when you see a host or hostess next after a dinner party or an event you were invited to. "Tack för tacket" is a phrase used once by a comedian, meaning "thank you for your thank you". Who said we are not polite? To "thank somebody" is "tacka", which could also mean "ewe". "Tack för nu", dear readers.

Tattoos

Sweden and the Scandinavian countries have the most tattooed inhabitants in the world, followed by the UK, Australia and China (2018).

A Swedish family visiting Mallorca, Spain, was asked by a waiter where they came from. "We are Swedish." He explained that the staff had been guessing. Since no member of the family had a (visible) tattoo, they could not quite make out what nationality they were. The only certain thing was that their guests were not Swedish.

Taube, Evert

Whenever someone throws a large party, you can bet the hosts will spice up the atmosphere by suggesting a sing-along. The sheets of papers that are distributed to all participants contain well-known melodies with new lyrics and ... a bunch of Evert Taube songs. This national poet and songwriter from Gothenburg wrote about his adventures on the high seas, in Argentina and in the Swedish archipelago. As an old man he shrewdly pretended to forget lyrics on stage, starting over again or talking about his life instead. On one occasion his wife started packing to leave him for good. Evert shouted "Wait for me" and started packing his belongings as well.

Telephoning

The division into area codes plays no vital role today. People use cell phones, so landlines have no importance. You will find no phone booths; they were abandoned years ago. The smartphone has taken over. Calling is on the whole fairly inexpensive. Facetime and Skype have added to this positive change.

Television

One television category consists mostly of programs where 10 people are in a competion, nine lose and have to go home, while the winner has 15 minutes of fame. It might include baking the most fantastic cake, singing better than others, cleaning your house better than anyone, trying farm life, surviving on a more or less deserted island or telling lies better than anyone else. (This last bit was a lie.)

Another popular category is "celebrities behaving like ordinary people" in programs where seven artists perform songs made popular by the other six, usually not quite as good as the original. Film stars, comedians and other personalities from the media spend days in a mansion talking about their lives, while chewing their food as they are speaking. In both shows silly games are included. (See TV!)

Thermometer scales

It takes a PhD in mathematics to get a grip on this conversion.

The freezing point in degrees Centigrade (Celsius) is 0, which corresponds to 32 degrees Fahrenheit. On a perfect summer day in Sweden, 80 degrees Fahrenheit would be a little less than 30 degrees in Centigrade. 60 degrees Fahrenheit equals 15 degrees Centigrade. If your child has a temperature, over a hundred degrees Fahrenheit, it will be about 40 degrees Centigrade.

F to C = (F − 32) x 5/9

C to F = C x 9/5 + 32

Threats to society

The Very Unofficial Guide to Heavy Stuff

Global changes caused by war, high oil prices, stock exchange slumps, starvation and dictatorships obviously affect Sweden. Domestic problems like the closure of factories, crisis in the IT-market, the Nasdaq-index (Stockholm Stock Exchange) going down and increasing unemployment, all have an impact on economy.

Thousands of employees "burning out" must be described as a new phenomenon. It arose in the 1990s and has been widely discussed and will continue to be. People not working for psychological reasons costs society huge sums of money, but most important, causes people a lot of pain.

Domestic and international criminals have joined forces and threaten the image of Sweden as a peaceful nation. Narcotics, trafficking, smuggling and the protection racket are expanding branches. Foreign outlaws operate in the country with or without their Swedish colleagues.

Time

It is important in Sweden. If you're invited at 7 p.m. you're expected at that time, not 15 minutes or an hour or two late as in a lot of other countries. People are known to have been circling the block of the party multiple times in their vehicle, because they have arrived a bit early. If a business meeting is scheduled for 2 p.m. it will start on the hour, possibly with one member arriving a bit late with a cup of coffee in his or her hand saying "sorry". Of course hen (= he or she) would have said it in Swedish. "Ursäkta mig." There would possibly be an explanation like "there was a flooding, my wife gave birth to a beautiful daughter, I was kidnapped by aliens" or "I forgot".

Tipping

According to the Swedish sense of equality, this remnant of the old days should not exist. You are not supposed to tip taxi drivers, hairdressers, bellboys (who do not exist in Sweden anyway) or porters at the railway station (who do not exist in Sweden either). We are all equals and who are you to throw a few coins at someone doing his job? Still, this feeling of all being equal makes a lot of people tip the waitress and the taxi driver, but not the bellboy who does not exist. After all, you think they deserve a few coins extra. Old people may even leave an envelope for the newspaperman or mailman at Christmas.

Titles

In the old days, say until 50-60 years ago, titles meant a lot. Doctor Helpless, Engineer Karlsson, Your Royal Highness, Vicar Andersson, Professor Smart and Aunt and Uncle Persson.

This last example shows the way children addressed neighbors. The latter ones would have been called Mr. and Mrs. Persson by their adult neighbors. Then, in the wake of the 60s revolution, we were told to dispense with titles. After all, we were all equals. Only first names were used. Today people have titles like Head of the Information Department, Director General of the National Board of Health and Welfare, Consultant for CAD Engineer, Senior Project Leader, Business Controller, External Communication Manager, Digital Media Designer and Key Analytics Group Manager Specialist. No Teachers, Nurses, Pilots or Smiths? And—did you notice—all in English. The more incomprehensible the title, the better status you have.

If you appear on television you are an expert: computer expert, rhetoric expert, social media expert. The only criterion is that you don´t have to rely on a specific education or degree. Professors or scientists on the other hand are merely professors or scientists.

Tourism in Sweden

Due to its geographical location, lots of non-European tourists prefer the continent or Britain instead of the North. Still, more than two million foreigners find their way to Sweden annually and their number is increasing. The largest groups of visitors are Norwegians and Germans. Danish and British guests are followed by Americans in the Top five (2018). Finnish, Dutch, French, Chinese and Japanese tourists also come in large numbers.

Towns

Swedish towns and other small places resemble nothing seen in English speaking countries. Due to the mass demolition of houses in the town centers, in the 1960s mainly, not much remains from earlier decades of the 20th century. Instead you will find modern boxes containing department stores and offices in many towns. Traffic is directed around the Swedish towns, and the long roads or streets with identical houses and front gardens and parked car in both directions cannot be seen either.

There are however towns in Sweden with partly or wholly preserved old town centers like Alingsås, Eksjö, Stockholm, Luleå Kyrkby and Visby (a medieval gem with a wall). Slum areas with no electricity or hot water ceased to exist many decades ago. Suburbs may have a bad reputation but hardly because they lack modern commodities.

Trade unions

Traditionally, trade unions hold a strong position in Sweden. Membership has gone down in recent years but at large companies and factories a majority of the employees often belong to a union. The Social Democrats, forming the majority of pre- and post-war Swedish governments, have encouraged this trend.

Traffic

In September of 1967 Sweden abandoned left-hand traffic and the population expected chaos. Nothing happened, though, except for the fact that the number of accidents drastically decreased. Trains still run on the right side which means to the left.

The honking of horns and obscene gestures do not play a major role. The Euro style, where dents and scuff marks on your vehicle show other motorists that you are a city person, does not apply in Sweden. You are supposed to curse other drivers, wishing they end up downstairs in a hot place, without moving your lips. Bite your lips and hiss the ugly words you do not expect your children to know. That is the civilized behavior expected from you.

Traffic rules may differ from your national ones. Speed checks are known to occur. Parking tickets may be fastened to your front window. Parking meters may be out of order and traffic lights have a tendency to turn red. Your headlights must be on 24 hours a day 365 days of the year, regardless of the midnight sun.

Even Christmas decorations all over won't stop that.

Any driver in a roundabout has reached stardom and must be given access. The four streets leading to the roundabout will soon be filled with drivers waiting with one foot on the accelerator. Still, they must wait. In the last few years the reintroduction of roundabouts has happened all over. They are supposed to be safe. The number of people killed in traffic does not usually exceed 250-280 per year (535 in 2002). Safe roads and other precautions have reduced the number, although traffic has increased considerably.

In the winter season (November–April) studded tires are used by many, be it dry, snowless or a blazing blizzard. Once on, they stay on. This costs the tax payers a lot, as studded tires destroy the road surface. This is probably the reason winter tires are gaining ground. These two types of tires are compulsory in the winter.

Keep your eyes open and you may see an Epatraktor, i. e. an old car transformed into a slow vehicle, with a young boy (always boys) in his "car" doing 20 mph.

Treriksröset

If you have never been to Scandinavia, try going to Sweden 11 times and Norway and Finland 10 times. All it requires is a walk of approximately 150 feet. It should take you about five minutes.

Treriksröset is situated in the north of the country in a bog. Norway, Finland and Sweden meet at exactly this point in the middle of nowhere. From the Finnish side you travel by boat across a rather big lake to reach Sweden. You have to walk for a mile until you get to a yellow monster of concrete in the middle of the bog. (Mind you, you will see a few more yellow look-alikes.) This is where the three countries meet. Walk around this monument and look at the plaques indicating which country is which. It is up to you how many times you want to visit each country. By the way, the thousands of mosquitoes that attack you are probably not Swedish.

Tricky Swedish words

Back: If you say "I want this back" you'd better point at a crate of beer. That is the meaning of the word.
- Barn: A barn contains hay or even cattle, but in Swedish the word simply means child or even children. "Take your barn to the zoo." Bairn in Scottish English.
- Bra: The Swedish population tends to use the word "bra" in all situations. Don't get alarmed, it is their way of saying "good," "fine" or "OK."
- Bye: It is a toilet word that describes the result of emptying your bowels. Do not even hesitate to say "bye, bye." The family's small children will love you. The spelling (baj) differs from the pronunciation.
- Fart: Come on. Don't be childish. It simply means speed. "At high speed" would be "with full speed" in Swedish. In other words "the plane took off with a terrible fart."
- Fart hinder: It corresponds to the English word for "sleeping policeman" or "speed bump."
- Godsexpedition: This is not a place of worship situated at an ordinary railway station but rather a service of the Swedish SJ (State Railways) where you can either hand in or collect goods sent to or from you. "Gods" is "goods" in Swedish.
- Gymnasium: You will see gymnasiums in each town or city swarming with teenagers aged 16 to 19. They usually carry their backpacks. Instead of sweaty sports shoes and damp towels these will contain torn math books and English text books or possibly history atlases or smart phones. Approximately 84% of this age group goes to upper secondary schools, which is "gymnasium" in Swedish as well as in German.
- Kiss: Here is another toilet word, which describes the fluid, which men produce standing and women sitting. By the way, men are encouraged to sit down to avoid the splish splash issue.
- Lo: the Swedish word for lynx may give you another impression of its meaning, but this beautiful and rare cat of which there are approximately 1,000 running wild, has been given the name "lo,"

not loo. If you happen to be looking for a loo, simply memorize the words "Allmän bekvämlighetsinrättning" and then look for the sign bearing the same letters in that order. If you urgently need to find a place of rest, then rather go for "toalett" or the female or male symbols. The long expression above is extinct today, so why look for it anyway? It might be translated as "general comfort facility."

- Sex: The idea of the Swedes being sexually active and frantically interested in this pleasure probably derives from the word "sex," which means "six" in Swedish. Someone probably wanted a six-pack of beer in some red district and said in poor English "Sex, please!" That's how it might have started. The Germans play the same game, "sechs."
- V.D.: What tends to be an infectious and hurtful disease in English, has a slightly more positive tone to it in Swedish. It means "managing director." To many Swedes the scandals with VDs and the so-called "parachute contracts" (golden handshakes) put them in the same category as any English VD though.
- Zoo: If you want a full-day excursion with your children, do not take them there (zooaffär is the full word). Twenty minutes will probably be enough to look around in this—pet shop. Nowadays the sign is not that common. If you want to go to a real zoo, look for the sign "Zoo" instead. If it looks like a large park with a high wall or a strong fence with an entrance, where you will have to pay, it is not a pet shop but a zoo. That is the difference.

Tubes

Do not be surprised to find porridge or brown beans in long transparent plastic tubes on display in the supermarket. Cheese, caviar (smoked red roe in "toothpaste tubs," mayonnaise, mustard, herbs, horseradish cream and mackerel in tomato sauce are examples of food that you can buy in tubes. These products are practical to carry along on a picnic, as they can be squeezed into any corner of a basket without getting broken. Just squeeze them and out comes a long string of goodies or, if you prefer, revolting stuff.

TV

Swedish public television (SVT), Channel 1 and 2, cost the paying viewer something like half a dollar per day. License fees made it possible to include classical concerts, literature debates, theatrical productions and non-commercial shows. Today the fees are included in the tax bill. TV 4 went from obscurity to stardom in the 1990s. This commercial channel, based on advertisements, concentrates on talk shows, series, films and entertainment.

For the majority of people who have fiber TV, the choice includes channels ranging from Asia to West Europe and America. CNN, BBC World, Discovery and VH1 and many more, make Sweden another TV-viewing nation. For any English-speaking visitor, Sweden must be a dream. Whenever you switch on the TV and start zapping you are most certainly guaranteed programs in English, from Australia, Canada, New Zealand, Britain, Ireland or the USA.

Swedish television, regardless of channels, believes in subtitles. Dubbing plays no role. Chinese, Italian, French or English programs have two lines at the bottom of the screen in Swedish. Problems arise when fast-speaking Americans or Italians make it impossible to include all the words at their speed of speech in the limited space in the lower part of the screen.

Television has probably played a great role in the Swedish interest in English, which in its turn has led to a high academic standard in speech and reading. A long, long time ago, in the 1980s, satellite dishes were introduced in a large suburb of Göteborg. It did not take long for teachers of English to notice that the ability to understand English, as demonstrated in the annual National Tests in schools, had gone up considerably in that part of the city. Swedes tend to love British series and British humor (see Humor). American talk shows and action films have a large following too. The other English-speaking countries of the world have also contributed to the success of Anglo-Saxon television.

Swedish teenagers probably know more about American murder trials than their Swedish equivalent ones. New York, the Big Apple, is familiar to most people and so are good old London and

[The] Swede

Sydney with its opera.

The American way of thinking in the production of films differs from Europe. We do not want clean, perfect faces in perfect bodies with faces lifted 10 times, and all in perfect upper class homes. Here ordinary people in ordinary situations are far more natural. The American habit of killing off a dozen or so people in action-comedies, whereas a normal female breast is regarded as porno, does not apply here. Rather one breast too many than a wasted life.

Treriksröset.

Uppland

This province, north of Stockholm and including parts of greater Stockholm, might be called the heart of Sweden. It is believed that Christianity spread from this part of the country, although other historians point out Västergötland in the west. In Uppsala kings were crowned and the University of Uppsala was founded in 1477.

Birka, an island in Lake Mälaren, west of Stockholm, was probably home to the oldest town in the country. It was an important trading post as early as the 9th century. Ansgar, the first missionary, arrived at Birka in 830 after having lost all his belongings traveling through this hostile land. More than 2,300 rock piles have been excavated. From Stockholm and Ekerö and other places you can get to Birka during the summer. Gamla Uppsala, north of Uppsala, is an old meeting place with the three "royal grave hills" and a medieval church. Uppsala is the most important town in the province. It houses the archbishop, and the cathedral can be seen from miles away. King Gustav Vasa is buried there. The university still plays a dominant role and has a very good reputation (number 73 worldwide in 2013).

Carl von Linné's Hammarby, near Uppsala, with his botanical garden, is worth a visit. Drottningholm, the royal home, has guided tours. Skokloster is another castle originating from the days of Sweden's great power in Europe (mainly the 17th century).

Sigtuna, founded in the 970s is the oldest existing town in Sweden. The church ruins dominate this picturesque little place where the main street is said to have been laid out in its present form 1,000 years ago. Other towns to visit include Vaxholm with the citadel, Enköping, an average small town with wood houses, Norrtälje near the water and Östhammar with its idyllic location. The old industries, dating back to the 17th century like Gimo bruk and Lövstabruk attract lots of tourists.

Vabba

This verb simply means to stay at home to care for a sick child and you are compensated economically. You stay at home from work and refrain from other forms of financial compensation. This is called temporary parental benefit. All you have to do is to fill in a form. An employer cannot refuse a parent to be at home with a child that really is ill (who has a fever, a rash or is coughing). If you misuse this right, you might be reported to the authorities.

The word "Vabruary" is an indication of the worst month of the year when children catch a cold or will have to see a doctor. Even grandmothers or grandfathers are entitled to help the child. But a retired person does not get economic compensation for natural reasons. He or she might get a cold instead. Vobba, another new phenomenon, means to work at home with a sick child.

Vacation

For tourists May and June can bring surprises. People still work and schools are open until June 6–15. The chances of getting a little sun at this time of year are favorable. It can even be as nice as in Italy or Spain ... almost! The tradition of choosing the rainiest month of the season, July, for vacation holidays remains strong, although the EU is about to change this habit. Every year disappointed nurses, clerks, engineers and masons return to work after having spent half the time inside their RVs or summer cottages to avoid showers or pelting rain.

SWEDEN CLOSED. GONE ON HOLIDAY or GONE FISHING would probably be the most common sign if ever there was one made. Do not expect to find small stores, garages, offices or sometimes even large companies open. Major supermarkets and department stores encourage some of their staff to work in July. Nurses have been known to get a much higher salary, if they save their holidays or part of it for some time other than July-August.

Swedes have at least five weeks of paid holidays. Families often save one week for the winter season in the mountains in February or at Easter. Others go for low season tickets to Mallorca, the Canary Islands or Cyprus and many simply stay at home.

Vasa, Gustav

King Gustav Vasa (1496–1560) overthrew the Danish king and defeated his troops who held control of Sweden. He returned from his exile in Lübeck, Germany, and started an uprising in Dalarna (a province). In 1523 Gustav Vasa became the king of Sweden, which then left the so-called Kalmar Union consisting of Denmark, Norway and Sweden. He ruled the country with an iron hand in order to get control over the provinces. Gustav made his subjects leave the Catholic Church, and Sweden became a Protestant Lutheran country. The belongings of the church were confiscated and transferred to the State.

The king was married three times. His family ruled the country until 1654 when Queen Kristina abdicated and decided to join a convent in Rome. By then Gustavus II Adolphus, her father, had already led his troops in the Thirty Years War. He was killed in the Battle of Lützen (Germany) in 1632. After his death his army eventually got as far as the Karl Bridge, Prague, the Czech capital today. The period 1611–1718 is called the Great Power Period. In those days Sweden included parts of current day Germany, Poland, Estonia, Latvia, Russia (the greater St. Petersburg area), part of Denmark and all of Finland.

An estimated number of 250,000 Swedes are described as part of the Vasa family (including in-laws). A series of three books was published in the fall of 2019 to make these people proud of being descendents of a tyrant that died in 1560. This writer is one.

Ven and Visingsö

These two islands, the first one between Denmark and Sweden and the second one in Lake Vättern, offer the tourist a full-day excursion with splendid views and swimming. To hire a bicycle on a sunny day in July and have a picnic is unbeatable. Ven is reached by boat from

Landskrona in the province of Skåne (Scania) and Visingsö by ferry from the town of Gränna, also a popular place with its famous Polkagris stick candy, just north of Jönköping.

Vikings

We refer to the period 800–1050 AD as the days of the Vikings. Whereas Norwegian Vikings mostly waged war on Ireland and Danish Vikings on England, when they were not raiding the rest of Western Europe, Swedish Vikings friendly exchanged goods in what is Russia today, and Belarus and the Ukraine.

The Swedish Vikings reached Novgorod, Smolensk and Kiev and today's Turkey. Some even got as far as Baghdad, the capital of Iraq. Slaves, weapons, wax, honey and fur were traded in exchange for silver coins, jewelry and cloth. Numerous books and other publications deal with the Vikings. Röde Orm, "Red Snake" by Frans G. Bengtsson is a classic novel, translated into English.

The observant reader would probably not agree with the words "Swedish Vikings friendly exchanged goods." Of course they were ferocious too. But at the same time the Vikings were smiths and artists, good craftsmen, forgotten talents in the description of them. And remember, their helmets were made of either iron or leather—with no horns. Also, the Vikings were simply a minority in the Scandinavian countries.

Visitors

Visitors from abroad are divided into two categories: 1) those from English-speaking countries, and 2) the rest. As for the first category, they can live in Sweden for 50 or even 70 years without speaking one word of Swedish. After 70 years it is too late anyway. The others are expected to speak perfect Swedish within months in order to qualify for jobs and be part of full integration in the Swedish society. By the way, the word "visitors" in this case is only a polite way of saying "immigrants" or "new Swedes".

Vägtull (Toll roads)

This irritating new phenomenon was introduced in Stockholm, later on in Göteborg (Gothenburg) as a means to handle the increasingly congested cities (and raise money). An electronic device scans the registration number on your vehicle, sends a bill to the owner and expects to be paid the correct sum. The price changes according to the time of day (like peak hours) you pass the cameras. Motorists with foreign registration numbers do not pay. A small number of bridges have the same system, although in this case they have fixed prices.

Värmland

The province of Värmland is known for its novelists and poets like Selma Lagerlöf and Gustav Fröding. This beautiful landscape with its long lakes and green forests invites you to the North, where Finns in the 16th and 17th centuries turned the forests into patches of farmland. Karlstad, the major town where the Swedish-Norwegian Union was dissolved in 1905, offers you a walk along Klarälven, the river with 165 miles of water in Värmland alone, or to the county museum near the water. The Sandgrund Lars Lerin Art Gallery offers fantastic watercolor and oil paintings, collages and photos by this giant artist.

Mårbacka, the mansion of Selma Lagerlöf, the laureate of the Nobel Prize in Literature, is open to the public. Ransäter with its Midsummer celebration and the play "Värmlänningarna," as well as the Rottneros mansion, are part of the history of Värmland. Places to see are Sunne, Torsby, Hagfors, Filipstad and Karlskoga.

Västerbotten

This province in the north was in previous centuries almost exclusively populated along the coast, except for the Sami people who stayed inland and to the west. During the last 400 years, the population has spread in a westerly direction, as ore and timber early became important products within the country.

[The] Swede

Gustav Vasa, Gustav 1, creator of what we see as Sweden, liberator although by the Danes of his time more likely considered usurper, possibly terrorist.

You get to Holmön, near Umeå, by ferry and there await cottages, bicycles for rent, cemeteries and prehistoric graves, all in beautiful surroundings. Buildings in Umeå, "the town of the birches," are built in wood with a considerable amount of space between them, all due to the fire that destroyed the town in 1888. The university attracts students from all over the country. Sävar (in today's Umeå) is where the last battle on Swedish soil was fought—against Russian troops in 1809.

Old Skellefteå with its church cottages and museums is worth a visit. The Pengsjö Settlers' Museum displays thousands of exhibits from centuries long gone.

Västergötland

The province of Västergötland, in western Sweden, offers a large plain with farms and small villages. There is a group of scholars who claim the origin of Sweden is to be found in Västergötland with all its medieval churches, ruins and buried kings. Olof Skötkonung, according to tradition, was the first Swedish king to be christened. This took place in Husaby, where the old church still stands. Officially, Uppland is said to be the cradle of the country.

In Västergötland, Ekornavallen offers impressive grave fields from prehistoric days. Hedared's chapel is the oldest preserved church of its kind. This wood building originates from the 1500s. Varnhem's klosterkyrka (monastery church) was founded by monks in the 12th century and today contains the remains of medieval royalty.

Läckö slott (castle) on a cape in Lake Vänern (the largest Swedish lake) is filled with busloads of tourists in the summer. From there you can go to the falls and locks of Trollhättan, lovely Skara with its cathedral and outdoor museum and the picturesque town of Hjo on Lake Vättern, and Göta Kanal, which traverses the province and then cuts through Sweden to the Baltic, receive thousands of visitors every year. Lidköping with the former Rörstrand's porcelain/china factories is worth visiting, like Borås with its zoo. Do not forget to stop at Ulricehamn, overlooking Lake Åsunden from the slopes.

Halle- and Hunneberg with their abandoned slate production and great fauna is a must for tourists arriving by car. Lake Hornborgasjön attracts up to 150,000 bird lovers every April when 10,000–20,000 cranes (the record 27,300) can be seen eating, dancing and sleeping. The Kinnekulle Mountain has existed for 500 million years and the tourist will need at least one day to enjoy all its beauty. Another day could easily be spent in the vicinity of Skara, at Sommarland (Summerland), the large adventure park with activities for the whole family. Karlsborg, on Lake Vättern, has an impressive fortress open to the public.

Västmanland

This is the land of ridges and iron, where man's activities date back to 1500 B.C. at least. Bergslagen is the name used for the area, where ore was extracted from the mountains. The region contains several old mines that can be visited. Kopparberg (Copper Mountain) invites visitors to its museums and workshops. This province offers charming little towns like Arboga with its old houses along the river and Sala with the silver mine and the major town of Västerås with Vallby open-air museum and much more. Anundshögsområdet, near Västerås, is a prehistoric field of graves and rune stones. Strömsholm's Canal runs through Fagersta and leads into Lake Mälaren and on to Stockholm. Strömsholm is also the name of a horse center. Hällefors boasts its steel- and timber industries.

Walks

"Walk round the block! What for?" the American cousins exclaimed. The poor old Oregon family, with Swedish guests, had no clue as to why anyone would want to behave in such an "un-American" way. Still, they guided their strange overseas cousins around the block and straight back to the house. The Swedes looked at each other in surprise and dismay. "That wasn't a walk? It took five minutes. A proper walk should take 45 minutes at a brisk pace."

This Swedish habit of walking your wife or husband, boy- or girlfriend, is like walking the dog in America. Many families have different rounds. They all lead back home, providing them with a reason to have a nice cup of coffee. After all, they have been so good.

If you come across people walking with ski poles, do not point at them. The Finnish started this new way of getting around looking like morons. Scientists claim that it has a positive effect on your lungs and heart. It stimulates your blood and gives you better exercise than ordinary walking. Old people often prefer this method. (See Stavgång!)

Wall–to-wall carpets

They were thrown out as early as the 70s. Most Swedes consider them to be unhealthy, collecting mites and dust. A clean, wooden floor that you can vacuum and see properly, offers advantages and faces no competition whatsoever.

Walpurgis Night (in Swedish Valborg)

On April 30, Swedes celebrate the arrival of spring. The traditional bonfires are lit in many places and people gather round them. In cities like Stockholm there will be male choirs singing about winter finally gone. The name Walpurgis, Valborg in Swedish, refers to a missionary who spread the word in Europe many, many centuries ago.

For students in the two university towns of Lund and Uppsala, this means celebration, starting with champagne breakfasts, later often changing into great street parties. In Uppsala homemade rafts make their way down the Fyris River before they collapse. Again, Sweden is full of surprise. Solemn celebration is mixed with fun and lots of beer.

West Coast, the

The West Coast, or the Best Coast as people of the area prefer to call it, consists of a band of little villages and islands that attract thousands of people in the summer. The former fishing villages, where the poor population lived in the first decades of the 20th century, are now inhabited by wealthy businessmen, IT-millionaires and stock exchange brokers, plus people who have inherited a house. The old fishermen's homes cost so much these days that no ordinary people can afford a house, no matter how small they are.

If you look out across the rocks, you will see a "freeway at sea" with large sail boats and huge motor boats going north or south in a never-ending line. The majority will fly the Swedish flag, followed by the Norwegian blue, white and red and the German black, yellow and red one. There will be Dutch and French boats too.

On land you will find visitors driving their cars through picturesque ex-fishing villages, stopping to take pictures of barren rocks and of course of their children. Nightlife in the tiny fishing villages along the Bohuslän Coast is hectic and not only young people, but also families with toddlers, will spend their evenings and money in restaurants and bars, forcing them to live on porridge for the rest of the year.

Windows

The English "window" derives from an Icelandic word that means "wind-eye." This was the hole on the roof where smoke left the dwelling and also cast some light to the interior in a dual-purpose way. In Sweden windows are double- or even triple glazed. They open outward in most cases. Do not attempt to pull them upward or down. It looks ridiculous actually.

Between the two panes you often find Venetian blinds that are controlled by a complicated set of strings and knobs. In homes you must not leave them down all day as that would mean shutting the light out and stopping people from admiring your window with the beautiful plants, which in their turn would die.

Young in Sweden

In an international survey many years ago they asked the question: "Where would a child lead the best life possible?" The answer was: "In the South Seas and in Scandinavia."

The rate of suicide in Sweden may contradict that statement. More people take their lives than people getting killed on the roads. A lot of suicide cases (roughly 400 under 30 years of age) happen among teenagers. Apart from this tragic statistic, young Swedes objectively have good lives. School tries to see the individual rather than the group. Physical abuse in homes is prohibited. Teenagers have a large amount of freedom. Economically average homes provide youngsters with more than the bare necessities of life.

The average young Swedes today are extroverted, easy-going, friendly and positive when you approach them. A French teacher once asked: "How come your students are so open-minded and sure of themselves?" Why not ask a Swede if this picture corresponds with reality? Opinions may differ.

Ångermanland

This province in the north has been inhabited for at least 4,500 years. Trade with the Sami people has always had high priority. It took Christianity quite a long time to get established in the valleys and the forests of Ångermanland. Anundsjö attracts tourists with its church and old farmhouses, all in the midst of lakes, forests and beautiful villages.

Härnösand is the "capital" of the province. With its large open-air museum and Vårdkasberget, a mountain with a splendid view, the town invites you to look at its buildings and sculptures. To the west of Gideå you will have an impressive view from the top of Böleberget (Mount Böle), which contains a huge cave more than 240 feet in length. Another mountain worth seeing is Skuleberget, which with its height of 960 feet and a national park, will give the tourist lots of opportunities to take exotic photos. Örnsköldsvik is a coastal town with beautiful buildings and another mountain (Varvsberget) with fantastic views.

At Junsele tourists gather for a music- and art week, unless they do some canoeing in the nature reserve. Nordingrå would probably be pronounced winner in popularity, if you asked visitors to Ångermanland to express their opinions. In this area you will find Högbondens fyr (a lighthouse), Bönhamn, a fishing village, and the low mountains and the many bays. If you would like to see a water power station, go to Nämforsen, where you may also experience the world of Stone Age people.

Öland

Sweden's second largest island is situated off the east coast of Småland in the Baltic. For nature lovers this is paradise. The mild and sunny climate, where fossils share the ground with fir trees and wetlands, has made it a popular gathering point for migrating birds. Boda kronopark is mainly covered by fir trees. Quite a number of rare plants and trees grow here. "Trollskogen" (trolls' forest), with its twisted oak and pine trees, gives it a spooky atmosphere. The treeless Alvaret (about 20 square miles) (See Alvar) with its variation of bushes, plants and herbs attracts tourists from all over.

The only town on the island is Borgholm, which is situated on ruins that go back to medieval days. Eketorps borg (a stronghold/fortress) has a wall surrounding the castle and the original is estimated to be 1,700 years old. Today Ekeborg is open to the public in the summer. Tourists may roam about among tame animals in the splendid replica of a castle. Many tourists go to see Långe Jan (a lighthouse) at Ottenby and also Solliden, the royal summer residence (like Balmoral in Scotland).

Öresundsbron

This amazing bridge connects Denmark and Sweden, at Copenhagen and Malmö, with its 5 miles (excluding the tunnel and the man-made island, another 5 miles) and is a fantastic landmark in the south. For tourists traveling by car to Sweden it means paying a toll before passing. The ride won't take long but on a clear day the view is splendid. The celebrated TV series "The Bridge" took place at and around it. Malmö, the next stop, is worth seeing. See it from a canal boat before continuing through the country.

Östergötland

This province of plains, lakes and archipelago will charm anyone wanting variation of sights. "That was the most interesting place so far," an English tourist exclaimed when he came to Norrköping. The flowing river and old factories, now turned into beautiful offices, shops and restaurants, made him say so. The trams also add to your well-being and peace. The neighboring town of Linköping, with its university and old town (Old Linköping) and museums with no entrance fees, simply has to be recommended, according to this English gentleman. The writer fully agrees.

The little town of Söderköping with Göta Canal and its locks is another nice stop and so are the (15) locks at Berg. Vadstena with its medieval convent (from 1384) on Lake Vättern should not be missed. Neither can Vreta Kloster (a nunnery primarily), nor Högbystenen, the old rune stone with the long inscription from the 10th century, which does not leave any visitor untouched. The most famous rune stone, however, Rökstenen (the Smokestone) from the 9th century, contains a text to the memory of a beloved son.

For families with children, Kolmården's Djurpark (zoo and safari park) is worth a full day. If caged animals or big mammals running free on the safari are not your cup of tea, Lake Tåkern offers nature lovers a chance to enjoy the number one spot for bird watching.

Översättning (Translation)

The following words will be found on signs all over the country.

Swedish noun with definite article	without	English
berget:	berg	mountain
borgen:	borg	castle, fort
byn:	by	village
bäcken:	bäck	brook, creek
dalen:	dal	valley
forsen:	fors	rapids
fästningen:	fästning	fortress, castle
gatan:	gata	street
hamnen:	hamn	harbor, port
kyrkan:	kyrka	church
köpingen:	köping	borough, small town
länet:	län	province, county
näset:	näs	minor peninsula, cape
platsen:	plats	place, location
sjön:	sjö	lake, sea
staden:	stad	town, city
sundet:	sund	strait, sound
torget:	torg	square
torpet:	torp	crofter's cottage
viken:	vik	bay
vägen:	väg	road
ån:	å	small river, creek
åsen:	ås	ridge
älven:	älv	river
ön:	ö	island

Christer Amnéus

Map of Sweden
including its 25 "Landskap" /
its old traditional provinces

This older division of Sweden has 25 regions. They are being used in this book and are often associated with tourism and native Swedes' sense of where they come from. And, let's face it, if you're visiting author Astrid Lindgren's birthplace, you're not going to Kronobergs Län, you're visiting Småland.

[The] Swede

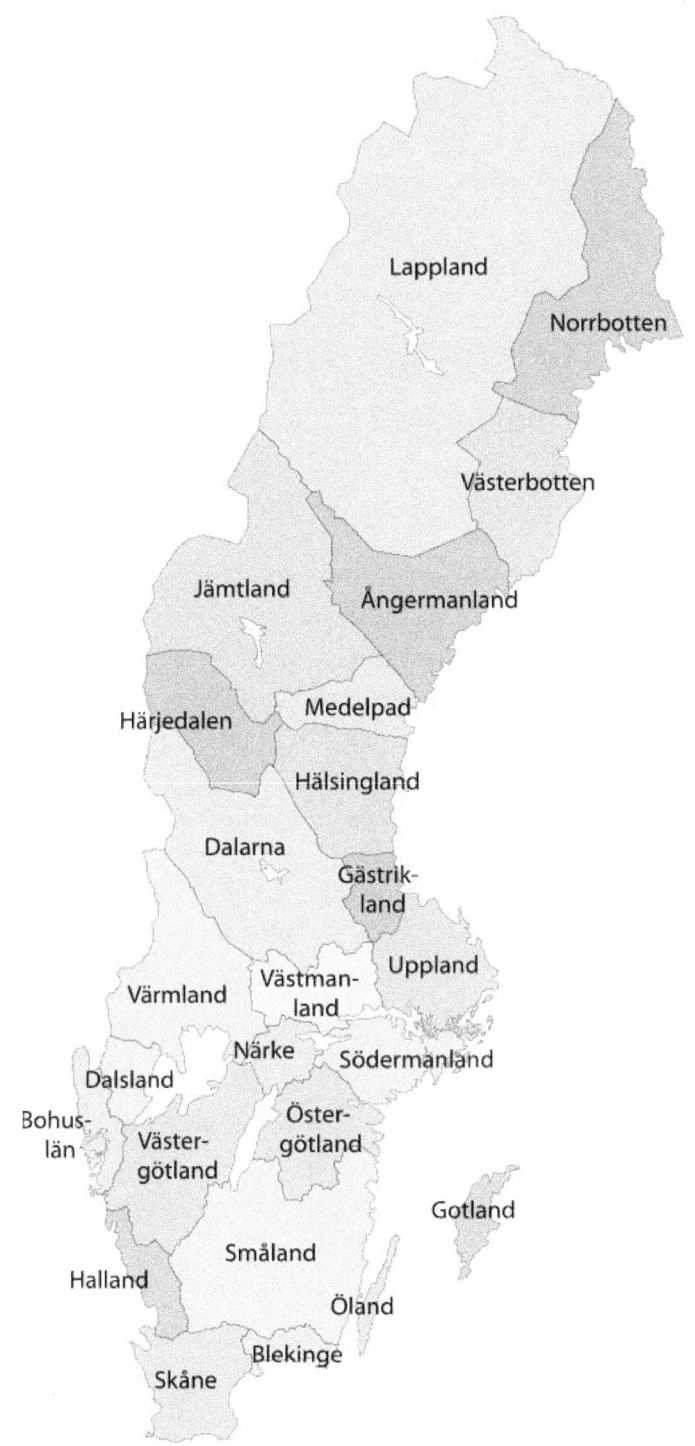

Christer Amnéus

Official map of Sweden
including the 21 "Län" / counties

The län are the top-level geographic subdivisions of Sweden. Compared to the provinces or "landskap" often referred to in the book and when talking to Swedes, the Lappland province is part of Norrbotten and Bohuslän, Västergötland and Dalsland make up Västra Götaland. Öland is part of Kalmar län (eastern part of Småland).

[The] Swede

Christer Amnéus

That's it.

Bye for now. Or rather ...

Hej då!

When you say goodbye, "Hej då" is the appropriate phrase. You could add "Vi ses" (See you later/soon). Old forms like "Farväl" or "Adjö" are as gone as cassettes or Dallas. If you want people to believe that you are matching Dagny Carlsson´s 107 years, then sure enough, otherwise no. Pronounce the phrase like "Hey door" but without the "r". Got it? Now, it is bye, bye to doors and hay. Instead, let´s move on in life so let´s say "Hej då" to these short lines. See you in Sweden, unless you are there already.

Christer Amnéus

[The] Swede

Addendum

Addendum

This section of the book is a list of the 100 most influential Swedes of the second millennium, developed by Nordstjernan for Sweden & America in December 1999. Text: Lars Henrik Ottoson, Ulf Barslund Martensson. Illustrations: Dave Granlund

The 100 Most Influential Swedes of the Millennium

It seemed so easy at first. Name the most noteworthy 100 Swedes of the last 1,000 years. We could rattle off at least 50 off the top of our heads. But who were the remaining 50? Wait a minute – did those first 50 come to mind because of their familiarity or fame, or because of their truly important achievements?

It is a question worthy of academic debate. Yet, despite our being neither professors nor scholars – possessing, in fact, no actual qualifications whatsoever for this task – we, the editorial staff at Nordstjernan dove right in anyway. We found the idea of the List a fascinating and thought-provoking challenge. Our criteria:

We chose people whom we felt have made such significant contributions to the country and the world that 100, even 200 years from now, they will still belong on the List.

We tried to pinpoint individuals whose achievements we believe could keep them on the List within their respective fields, say, to the year 3000, if such a date is possible.

Addendum

We chose only people whose contributions are being felt here and now, the present day. Who knows: If Ingvar Kamprad truly does furnish the world or Erling Persson of Hennes & Mauritz dresses it, surely they will make it onto the List in a thousand years... Well, twenty years after completing the list, now in 2020, we can rightfully admit, they will. In 1999, H&M was planning to open its first store on American soil—a prime location on Fifth Avenue set to open in March 2000. There are now over 500 stores all across the U.S. Similarly, it seems IKEA is furnishing the world. From under 30 stores in North America in 2000, the home products company now has 67 and has become known for innovatively recreating the way we see, choose and evaluate our home designs in the future.

The world has changed in many ways throughout these twenty years and many other names would surely have ended up in the final section, "Also considered." The most potentials may be under the world of business, musicians and possibly stage and screen. Skype, the online communications tool, originally launched in 2003 and cofounded by Niklas Zennström or audio streaming platform Spotify, founded by Daniel Ek and Martin Lorentzon in 2006 would be natural contenders under business. If Abba has had a follower in the world of music it would be Roxette, the duo with Per Gessle and the late Marie Fredriksson. Swedish House music has created several world names, Swedish House Mafia and the late Tim Bergling, better known as Avicii, among them. Among songwriters and producers Max Martin, who's the songwriter with the third-most number-one singles on the Billboard Hot 100 chart, behind only Paul McCartney and John Lennon. Several Swedish directors along with actors have also made it internationally over the last 20 to 30 years. The director Lasse Hallström's second Oscar nomination for The Cider House Rules was in 1999 but his works have been celebrated both before and after this nomination. Will climate activist Greta Thunberg become a historical heavyweight and show up in history books 200 years from now? It's 2020 and right now it seems likely but who knows what the next 100 years will bring? And of course, in sports, how can anyone overlook Swedish international soccer star Zlatan Ibrahimowic?

Any list of this kind is controversial by definition and will no doubt provoke discussion and disagreement. No one can argue the impact that the Viking, Engelbrekt and King Gustav Vasa have had on Sweden and the world. But some learned folk might question us on our selection and ranking of those we see as the 20 most important figures in Sweden's millennial history. There are also fewer women on the List than we would like – a function of history's selective exclusion of women's accomplishments. However, we feel we can defend our choices.

When it came to the second 80, we took an easier way out by listing those individuals chronologically within their respective fields of endeavor. After all, is it really fair to pit Greta Garbo against Karl XIV Johan or weigh Harry Martinsson against Anna Maria Lenngren in terms of relative worth?

Let the original List begin. Håll till godo.

Ulf Barslund Martensson, December, 1999 and January, 2020.

Addendum

The hall of twenty

1. **Alfred Nobel (1833 – 1889)**
   Inventor of dynamite whose name will live forever through the Nobel Prizes.

2. **John Ericsson (1803 – 1896)**
   Engineer who revolutionized shipping by inventing the propeller; during the U.S. Civil War, he built the iron-clad "Monitor" and saved the Union fleet at Hampton Roads.

3. **Gustav II Adolf (1594 – 1632)**
   His defeat of the Catholic armies saved Protestantism in Europe; under his rule, Sweden became Europe's mightiest and largest nation.

4. **Gustaf Dalén (1869 – 1937)**
   His invention, the sun vent, still runs lighthouses and marks shipping lanes around the world. Nobel Prize winner in physics, 1912.

5. **Carl von Linné (1707 – 1778)**
   His system of binomial nomenclature scientifically classified plants and animals.

6. **Jöns Jakob Berzelius (1779 – 1848)**
   Influential chemist who introduced modern chemical symbols and formulae.

7. **Carl Willhelm Scheele (1742 – 1786)**
   A founder of organic chemistry, he identified oxygen, nitrogen, manganese, barium, molybdenum and wolfram.

8. **Christopher Polhem (1661 – 1751)**
   Creator of the world's first padlock and universal joint, the so-called "Polhemsknuten."

9. **Anders Celsius (1701 – 1744)**
   Astronomer who gave the world the centigrade temperature scale.

10. **August Strindberg (1849 – 1912)**
    One of the world's great dramatists and authors.

11. **Emanuel Swedenborg (1688 – 1772)**
    An engineering genius, philosopher and mysticist, his revivalist movement still has adherents in the U.S.

12. **Sven Hedin (1865 – 1952)**
    Legendary explorer who discovered the Trans-Himalaya, traced the source of the Brahmaputra River and mapped large unknown areas of Tibet.

13. **Jenny Lind (1820 – 1887)**
    The Swedish Nightingale's memory lingers 150 years after her last concert.

14. **Jussi Björling (1911 – 1960)**
    Along with Enrico Caruso, considered by many to be the greatest operatic tenor of all time.

15. **Raoul Wallenberg (1912 – ?)**
    The "hero of Budapest" saved thousands of Jewish lives during the Second World War and subsequently disappeared in the Soviet Union. Only the second-ever honorary U.S. citizen (after Winston Churchill), a statue was raised in his honor on Washington, D.C.'s Capitol Hill.

16. **Dag Hammarskjöld (1905 – 1961)**
    Influential Secretary General of the United Nations and recipient of the Nobel Peace Prize, 1961.

17. **Anders Jonas Ångström (1814 – 1874)**
    A dominant figure in spectroscopic analysis, he developed wave-

length classifications for the solar spectrum (angstrom units).

18. Olof Rudbeck the older (1630 – 1702)
Perhaps the most versatile scientist in Swedish history; publisher of Atland or Manheim, about Atlantis. In "proving" that Sweden was the world's first cultivated region, considered a masterpiece, combining both deeper scientific knowledge with fictional writing.

19. Archbishop Nathan Söderblom (1866 – 1931)
Prominent church leader and recipient of the Nobel Peace Prize, 1939.

20. Fredrika Bremer (1801 – 1865)
Writer who fought for women's rights and founded the Swedish suffrage movement.

Historical heavyweights

The Viking (800 – 1050)

Engelbrekt Engelbrektsson (d. 1436)
Freedom fighter who battled the Danes and instilled a national Swedish spirit.

Gustav Vasa (1496 – 1560)
He drove out the Danes: the founder, father and first king of a united Sweden.

Karl X Gustav (1622 – 1660)
Brought the provinces of Skåne and Blekinge under Swedish rule.

Karl XII (1682 – 1718)
The nemesis of Russia's Peter the Great, he lost his troops to the Russian winter and reduced Sweden from great European power to historical footnote.

The Holy Birgitta (1303 – 1373)
After her pilgrimage to Rome, she founded the Vadstena convent, home to the still-active Birgitta Order.

Axel Oxenstierna (1563 – 1654)
Someone had to run Sweden while the kings were at war—Oxenstierna did it well, and is remembered as one of the nation's finest statesmen.

Queen Kristina (1626 – 1689)
The daughter of Gustav II Adolf and Sweden's last reigning queen, her conversion to the Catholic faith, abdication and subsequent move to Rome remain one of the greatest triumphs of the Roman Catholic Church.

Gustav III (1748 – 1792)
King who brought the Swedish court on par with European royal houses, spending lavishly on arts and splendor. Crossing the country's nobility got him assassinated during a masquerade ball, an event dramatized in Guiseppe Verdi's opera "Un Ballo en Maschera."

Johan Banér (1696 – 1641)
Commander of the victorious Swedish forces at Wittstock and Chemnitz, and governor of Pomerania.

Carl Gustaf Wrangel (1613 – 1676)
A general at 24, he was commander of the fleet and field marshal of the victorious Swedish army at Warsaw in 1656.

Karl XIV Johan (1763 – 1844)
The first of the Bernadottes, Napoleon's field marshal became Sweden's first modern king and actively contributed to Napoleon's defeat and fall.

Adolf Erik Nordenskiöld (1832 – 1891)
Explorer who discovered the Northeast Passage around Siberia to the Bering Strait.

Folke Bernadotte (1895 – 1958)
Humanitarian who organized Red Cross refugee relief expeditions at the end of the Second World War, he was murdered by terrorists during a mission to Israel.

Carl Gustaf von Rosen (1908 – 1977)
Humanitarian, adventurer, aviator who flew relief missions in Africa and was a one-man air force during the Nigerian war. Killed by Somali guerillas.

The literati

Carl Michael Bellman (1740 – 1795)
Sweden's timeless master balladeer, his works remain the repertoire of troubadours and school choirs.

Anna Maria Lenngren (1754 – 1817)
Was there before or since any Swede with her knowledge, common sense and literary genius? Poet, translator and author, often considered a pioneering female activist.

Johan Olof Wallin (1779 – 1839)
Archbishop and composer behind the modern Swedish Lutheran hymnal, to which he contributed 140 hymns of his own, including "Var hälsad sköna morgonstund."

Esaias Tegnér (1782 – 1846)
Poet, patriotic writer and bishop, his Fritjofs Saga was translated into every language in Europe. His lyrical sense language has never been surpassed in Swedish poetry.

Carl Jonas Love Almqvist (1783 – 1866)
Romantic poet, early feminist, realist, composer, social critic, and traveler, a prolific social satirist considered by many to be the first modern Swedish writer.

Lars Hierta (1801 – 1872)
Writer, journalist and publisher, he founded Sweden's first daily newspaper, Aftonbladet, in 1830. His publishing house pioneered the production of low-cost editions of famous works, so-called shillingtryck, the paperbacks of their time.

Viktor Rydberg (1828 – 1895)
Novelist and religious philosopher who nonetheless is best remembered for creating the timeless tale of the Tomten: "Midvinternattens köld är hård, stjärnorna glimma och gnistra ... endast tomten är vaken."

Selma Lagerlöf (1858 – 1940)
Author of the unforgettable "Adventures of Nils Holgersson and first recipient of the Nobel Prize in Literature, 1909.

Werner von Heidenstam (1859 – 1940)
Poet and novelist, laureate of the Nobel Prize in Literature in 1916.

Gustaf Fröding (1860 – 1917)
Complex and tormented poet whose work was beloved by many. When his demons finally felled him, his tombstone read, "Det borde vara stjärnor att pryda ditt änne"—There should be stars to adorn your forehead.

Erik Axel Karlfeldt (1864 – 1931)
Recipient of the Nobel Prize in Literature, 1931.

Hjalmar Söderberg (1869 – 1941)
Author of some of Sweden's most-read modern novels, including "Dr. Glas" and "Martin Birck's Youth."

Albert Engström (1869 – 1940)
Incomparable humorist, artist, illustrator and writer; the creator of Kolingen and Rospiggen.

Hjalmar Bergman (1883 – 1931)
Perhaps Sweden's best storyteller of all time.

Pär Lagerkvist (1891 – 1874)
Recipient of the Nobel Prize in Literature, 1951.

Frans G. Bengtsson (1894 – 1954)
An author who found adventure in history and told it like no one else, as in "Röde Orm."

Wilhelm Moberg (1898 – 1973)
An icon in Swedish literature for his classic story of Swedish emigrants to America and his History of the Swedish People.

Nils Ferlin (1898 – 1961)
The Bellman of modern Sweden, an "everyman's" poet.

Eyvind Johnsson (1900 – 1976)
and Harry Martinsson (1904 – 1978)
Co-recipients of the Nobel Prize for Literature, 1974.

Astrid Lindgren (1907 – 2002)
The world's master of children's books and creator of Pippi Longstocking.

Stage and screen

Christina Nilsson (1843 – 1921)
Leading European soprano and star of the Metropolitan Opera.

Victor Sjöström (1879 – 1960)
Character actor and stage and movie director, he was one of the pioneers of Hollywood's silent-movie era.

Warner Oland (1880 – 1938)
Born Verner Ölund, he has perhaps been seen on television more times than any other Swede—albeit better known as Charlie Chan.

Lars Hansson (1886 – 1965)
One of Hollywood's finest dramatic actors and co-star of Greta Garbo.

Mauritz Stiller (1893 – 1929)
The genius who brought Greta Garbo to Hollywood and made some of the silent-movie era's masterpieces.

Evert Taube (1890 – 1976)
A Swedish "national treasure" and beloved troubadour.

Greta (Gustafsson) Garbo (1905 – 1990)
The legendary, mysterious and divine Miss G.

Ingrid Bergman (1915 – 1983)
Seeing the movie "Casablanca" at least once should be required by law.

Ingmar Bergman (1918 – 2007)
No introduction necessary for the legendary film director.

Nicolai Gedda (1925 – 2017)
Swedish tenor followed in the footsteps of Jussi Björling. Performed in opera houses around the world but felt best at home at the Metropolitan.

ABBA (1972 –)
The music of Benny Andersson's and Björn Ulvaeus' creation continues to capture the world. ABBA remains the all-time leading record-selling group, topping even the Beatles.

The musicians

Wilhelm Pettersson Berger (1867 – 1942)
Romantic poet and composer as well as much-feared music critic for Stockholm's Dagens Nyheter. Best known for his piano suite "Frösöblomster."

Wilhelm Stenhammar (1871 – 1927)
Conductor and symphony composer whose "Sverige" is still one of the most powerful pieces written for male chorus.

Hugo Alfvén (1872 – 1960)
His "Midsommarvaka" may be the Swedish orchestral composition most commonly played outside of Sweden.

Karl Birger Blomdahl (1916 – 1968)
Sweden's most talented and versatile modern composer, with a range including symphonies, chamber music and opera.

Sixten Ehrling (1918 –2005)
A "conductor's conductor," he has led the Stockholm Opera and Detroit Symphony, and served as head of the orchestra and conducting at New York's Julliard School of Music. Does he really belong on the top 100? When people like Dan Andersson and Povel Ramel are exluded? I question this one.

The artists

Carl Larsson (1853 – 1919)
A watercolor print of one of his rural family scenes can be found in the home of almost every Swede abroad.

Anders Zorn (1860 – 1920)
His portraits and nudes made him Sweden's most internationally acclaimed painter.

Bruno Liljefors (1860 – 1939)
As a wildlife painter Liljefors, had no equal.

Carl Milles (1876 – 1955)
Milles' Memorial Garden draws sculpture lovers from around the world.

Addendum

The wide world of sports

Ulrich Salchow (1877 – 1949)
This world figure skating champion (1901-1907) and Olympic gold medalist (1908) is commemorated every time one sees a skater doing a double or triple Salchow.

Erik Lemming (1880 – 1930)
World record-holding javelin thrower with four Olympic gold medals and 25 Swedish championships.

Gillis Grafström (1893 – 1938)
Few have dominated a sport as he dominated figure skating: he reigned undefeated through three consecutive Olympics and the world championships of 1922 to 1928.

Arne Borg (1901 – 1987)
Olympic gold-medalist swimmer and holder of 30 world records.

Gunder Hägg (1918 – 2004)
Long-distance runnerWonder Gunder held every world record from 1500 meters to 5000 meters between 1941 to 1945.

Gert Fredriksson (1919 – 2006)
King of the canoes and winner of six Olympic gold medals and four world championships, his fellow Olympians voted him the world's most outstanding athlete in 1957.

Sixten Jernberg (1929 – 2012)
The world's foremost winter Olympian and one of the most successful cross-country skiers of all time, he won nine Olympic medals and four world championships in cross-country skiing.

Ingemar Johansson (1932 – 2009)
World heavyweight boxing champion in 1959. His championship match with American Floyd Patterson was watched or heard by people around the world.

Ingemar Stenmark (1956 –)
One of the world's best-ever alpine skiers, a repeat world, Olympic and World Cup champion.

The politicians

Hjalmar Branting (1860 – 1925)
Led the Social Democratic party into power and became the party's first prime minister. Recipient of the Nobel Peace Prize, 1921.

Per Albin Hansson (1885 – 1946)
Prime minister credited with creating Sweden's modern welfare state, or "det svenska folkhemmet."

Gunnar Myrdahl (1898 – 1987)
The intellectual and financial brain of the Social Democrats and a world-renowned economist whose works were standard reading at U.S. universities. Recipient of the Nobel Prize in economics, 1974.

Ernst Wigforss (1881 – 1977)
Created with Per Albin Hansson Sweden's system of progressive taxation, the economic bedrock of the welfare system.

Tage Erlander (1901 – 1985)
Prime minister from 1946 to 1969, he furthered social-reform politics and introduced full health coverage and the present-day pension-fund system.

Olof Palme (1927 – 1986)
Sweden's internationally most recognized—but also most controversial, even disliked—prime minister. The only political figure in Sweden in modern times to be assassinated.

The world of business

Axel Johnsson (1844 – 1910)
Founded the Nordstjernan shipping line (a few years after the newspaper Nordstjernan) and took over the Avesta Iron Works, starting one of Sweden's largest the industrial conglomerates.

Karl Otto Bonnier (1856 – 1941)
Patriarch of the Bonnier family dynasty, which dominated the Swedish publishing and newspaper world. Today, over 50 percent of Swedish publications originate in a Bonnier company.

Carl Edward Johansson (1864 – 1945)
Also known as "Mått" (Measure) Johansson, he built his company on his invention of a gauge-block measuring instrument capable of previously unknown precision. For many years was one of Henry Ford's closest associates.

Sigfrid Edström (1870 – 1964)
He turned ASEA into Sweden's largest industrial company; also served as chairman of the International Olympic Committee.

Sven Wingquist (1876 – 1963)
Founded SKF, the world's largest ball-bearing manufacturer, on his invention, the double-row, self-aligned ball bearing.

Ivar Kreuger (1880 – 1932)
Legendary industrialist who controlled 75 percent of the world's match industry, he was a venture capitalist 60 years before the term was coined. Financed much of Sweden's modern industry, as well as

making huge loans to the government Germany and France. Upon his suicide, thousands of Swedes and people all over the world lost everything financially.

Axel Wenner Gren (1881 – 1961)
Founder of Electrolux and one of the world's richest and most powerful individuals in the 1950s and 1960s, with global companies and holdings. Remembered as a generous supporter of science.

Sven Salén (1890 – 1969)
Created a shipping line and pioneered the transportation of perishable fruit with cold storage ships—at one time, every banana in the world was shipped by Salén.

Jakob Wallenberg (1892 – 1980)
Led the Wallenberg industrial empire from 1927 to 1960. Competes on this list with his brother Marcus, grandfather of the present Wallenberg patriarchs, two cousins, Marcus and Jakob.

Ruben Rausing (1895 – 1983)
The founder of TetraPak made himself and his kin among the world's richest families.

Also considered

Who almost but didn't make the List? Decide for yourself if any of these individuals should have made the Top 100 Most Influential Swedes of the Millennium List. Remember, though, if you want to put one in, you have to take another one out.

Historical heavyweights: Torgny Segerstedt, The (Theodor) Swedberg

Literati: Dan Andersson, Bo Bergman, Johan Henrik Kellgren, Ellen Key, Fritiof Nilsson Piraten, Sigfrid Siwertz, Birger Sjöberg,

Carl Snoilsky, George Stiernhielm, Erik Johan Stagnelius, Elin Wägner. Karin Boye? What about later names such as Sjöwall-Wahlöö, Henning Mankell or Stieg Larsson—well read with volumes of books sold but, literary giants? You decide.

Stage and screen: Alice Babs, Povel Ramel, Ernst Rolf, Max von Sydow, Anders de Wahl. What about Nils Poppe? Or the more recent Noomi Rapace, who portrayed Lisbeth Salander in the Swedish film adaptations of the Millennium series ... the Emmy award winning Alexander Skarsgård or his father Stellan, who won an Emmy in 2020 for his role in the mini series Chernobyl ... or the 2016 Oscar winner Alicia Vicander?

Politicians: Alva Myrdahl, Fabian Månsson, Karl Staaff, Gunnar Sträng.

Sports: Björn Borg, Gre-No-Li, Mora Nisse Karlsson, Pehr Henrik Ling, Patrik Sjöberg, Nacka Skoglund, Sven Tumba. How about Gunde Svan?

Artists: Carl Eldh, Johan Sergel

Business: Holger Crafoord (Gambro), Gunnar Engellau (Volvo), Axel Ax:son Johnsson (Nordstjernan), Ingvar Kamprad (Ikea), Carl Fredrik Liljevalch (Grängesberg), Erling Persson (H&M).

***

If you liked this book you may want to stay informed of other
things going on in the Swedish and Swedish American community
in the U.S. – the easiest way is with a subscription to Nordstjernan –
America's oldest, yet contemporary Swedish periodical,
a tradition since 1872. A subscription will pay for itself through
the special offers you are eligible for. Call 800.827.9333
or see a sample of content at *www.nordstjernan.com*

Other books we publish: *www.nordicsampler.com*.

www.ingramcontent.com/pod-product-compliance
Lightning Source LLC
Chambersburg PA
CBHW061257110426
42742CB00012BA/1959